EMILIO GRECO SCULPTURE & DRAWINGS

JP HODIN

Adams & Dart, Bath

First published in 1971 by
Adams & Dart, 40 Gay Street, Bath, Somerset

SBN 239 00052 8

Designed by Barry Robson
Printed in Italy by Alfieri & Lacroix, Milan
Bound in Great Britain

Contents

References in the text to monochrome illustrations are indicated by the number, in parenthesis, of the illustration in bold type, while the colour plates are given in roman figures, also in parenthesis

Preface

Beauty should never be presented, explained. It is Marvel and Wonder, and in art we should find first these doors – Marvel and Wonder – and, coming through them, a slow understanding (slow even though it be a succession of lightening understandings and perceptions) as of a figure in mist, that still and ever gives to each one his own right of believing, each after his own creed and fashion.

Always the desire to know and to understand more deeply must precede any reception of beauty. Without holy curiosity and awe none find her, and woe to that artist whose work wears its 'heart on its sleeve'.

Ezra Pound

Of Beauty

There is a view-point beyond all specialised and fragmentary ways of approach in art – a view-point in which they are all united, in which they all receive and conserve their true meaning, the meaning which we call the philosophy of art. And Beauty can play its part not as an historically established notion but as a necessary corrective of all the rationalistic and nihilistic attitudes of today, be it the concept of life's mechanisation, of absurdity, or of Angst, the destructive urge, the regression to primitivism or the gospel of ugliness: Beauty as nostalgia out of our hell, the enigma of perfection in the sense of Kant's Transcendent Beauty, or, as the prophetic woman spoke to Socrates of Man in search of Beauty in the Symposium: He will begin 'with the love of beautiful things and continuously ascending, as though by steps, for the sake of Beauty itself, from one beautiful body to two and from two to all and from beautiful bodies to beautiful morals and from beautiful morals to beautiful sciences and from sciences finally to that science which is nothing less than the science of pure Beauty, wherein the true essence of Beauty is learnt! Therein, my dear Socrates, if anywhere, should life be lived'.

Perhaps the search for Beauty calls for a force great enough to recognise a higher and deeper meaning in and beyond our time's obscurities of existence, the tragic conflicts and hateful abysses. What is at stake is not an ideal but a force which refines and elevates. Only he who loves can see Beauty, and only he who loves can truly create. Braque, when asked about the problem of Beauty, said to me during a conversation in the summer of 1952: 'There is first the question whether Beauty is a problem. It is not because there are no fixed data. Such data are misleading. There is no solution for life – there is, however, a perpetual process of adaptation. I have replaced the notion of the Eternal by the idea of the Perpetual. The question of Beauty is a question of achieving harmony. And harmony is nothingness for the intellect, where words have no value. It is a state of grace or of mystic illumination. In such a state one comprehends Beauty.'

J P Hodin

* * * * * *

May I take this opportunity of here expressing my gratitude to the artist for his unfailing friendship and his generous co-operation in putting at my disposition all the information needed for the completion of the story of his life and the development of his art, as well as for providing the illustration material used in this volume. I am indebted to my wife, Pamela, for her untiring and conscientious help in checking the text; to Dr Arch Torquato Terracina, for important details concerning the doors of Orvieto and their history; to the public and private owners of the sculptures and drawings reproduced in this monograph; to Anna Greco, the artist's wife, for her assistance in providing important material, and to Mr Antony Adams, for his enthusiasm for and care in producing this book.

May this book prove to be one of those of which William Wordsworth wrote:

'Dreams, books are each a world; and books we know
Are a substantial world, both pure and good.
Round these, with tendrils strong as flesh and blood,
Our pastime and our happiness will grow.'

JPH

The Swan Song of Europe

'Swans sing before they die'
Coleridge

Europe in the minds of the thoughtful was one of the most exciting dreams of mankind striving for clarity, for beauty and meaning – fullness, a dream of the perilous and prolonged struggle for man's dignity, for his soul in its unique dimensions, for his personality and freedom, for the quest of becoming human with moral, aesthetic and cognitive standards highly established, ever changing and nevertheless remaining the same, unfolding though perpetually moving in that one direction only designed for it by its destiny (not its history) and thus accomplishing the complex pattern of its inner needs and beliefs. So arose that grand panorama which is Europe before our eyes, the Europe we know, with its precious buildings and human aspirations, the treasure houses of its old cities, its libraries, churches, palaces and chapels, with its scent of the past and the promise of the future, the Europe of Herodotus, who wrote the first history of the world known to antiquity, and Homer, who wrote the first Greek mythology, who also described for the first time the fate of an individual, Ulysses; the Europe of that sculptor who for the first time reported the face of man. 'You know the head of the young man in the Acropolis Museum?' asked André Malraux in *Les Noyers de l'Altenbourg*. 'The first sculpture to have represented the *human face*: free of monsters, of death, of the gods. . . .'[1]

And here too were those seekers for God the Creator, who for the first time took up the challenge in writing down the unchangeable laws of justice and of good will followed by the promise of an eternal life, the vision of a last judgement, of Heaven and Hell, of man's redemption and spiritualisation, the humanisation of nature.

Greek myth, philosophy and science, the concept of life as a godlike presence with no reference to any transcendental power, stood at the cradle of the Christian church, which started its flight still weighed down by the exclusiveness and pride of the Synagogue. They penetrated each other's sphere of belief. They fought and supported each other. In the monasteries, the old Greek wisdom was preserved, and when the beauty of its humanism came into the open in its old strength, during the 14th century, and the sudden and even violent discovery of its arts was like a ray of light in the dark – for mediaeval man had forgotten its sunlike glory – a new step was taken forward in the formation of European man, his rebirth, his 'Renaissance'. And as we find roots from Egypt and the Near East in Greek beliefs and art forms, so also we find Moresque patterns in architectural elements brought by the Crusaders to the North and West in Gothic times when European man prayed anew and most intensely to his God of inner brightness, his Saviour.

[1] Gallimard, nrf. Paris 1941.

Oh, this enigmatic and puzzling smile on the female faces of Minoan wall paintings and of early Greek pots and sculptures. Is it not the same which appears again, but gentler now and sweeter in the looks of Gothic saints after all that oppressive and apocalyptic gloom of the Romanesque age? A Greek Christian Symbiosis, the reconciliation of opposites creating a new unity, the tolerance and acceptance of both, the wordly and the other worldly, the permanent and the transitory, Dante and Bocaccio, Michelangelo and Raphael. And again the smile and the beauty of the face of Bernini's *St Theresa* appears two centuries later, and three centuries later we find it in the sweetness of Renoir's young womanhood. Another hundred years and we stand before Emilio Greco's sculptures of '*Il Bagnante*' (The Bather). At the time when Greco staged his first Bagnante, Professor Erwin Schrödinger discovered the sources of modern science in Greek thought.[1]

All these manifestations, the Greek and Jewish-Christian heritage, the scrupulous and self-analysing mind of Montaigne, the Pantheistic Credo of Spinoza, Goethe's Iphigenia, Hermann and Dorothea, the second part of his Faust, his Orphic songs, the poetry and thought of Nietzsche, they all have one source only, the source of European culture: The Mediterranean. Here are the roots of all its beauty, its morals, its philosophy, its science. And here too was the home of those who knew how to conquer and organise Europe in the name of law and order. They built its roads, aqueducts, and fortifications, brought sport and hygiene to the backward lands and with it the knowledge of Greek and Roman thought.

How did it come about that none of the nations of Europe could achieve what the Romans had been able to achieve, giving as they did a firm basis to European civilisation in the wake of which Christendom could spread far into the cold North? Why should all this heritage now be regarded as a most doubtful blessing, to be renounced in the suicidal attempt at alienation which is inherent in the adoption of Africa as the source of a rejuvenating process in art, in music, in primitive sexualism, proclaiming the ugly beautiful and sophistication degenerate? Why should the peaks of our achievement be devalued for the sake of some fanciful never-to-be-achieved elementarism? Why all this brutalisation of human relationships, this wallowing in mud, this belief in the absurdity of life, this Existentialist Nihilism, this flight from the visible and tangible into abstraction, from the sacred into banality?

Because we have become the victims of Science and Technology in thought and action and are afraid of ourselves.

Why do we bury Europe which had all the means of enlightening mankind, and even bridging the abyss between Western and Eastern culture?

Because we no longer believe in man as a whole, only in the animal side of his being and the products of his ratio.

Why have we replaced the natural reasoning of our minds, our pride as holders of a venerable heritage, our role as pathmakers in the present chaos?

Because we have unleashed the powers of nature's innermost secrets without being able to control them. In the roar of our machines we no longer hear the low voice of Creation, the call of our hearts. We are entangled in fear and aggression, we have no reverence for life because we believe that we have discovered the functioning of some hereditary mechanism. We do not recognise the necessity of art because we believe only in reason. We are 'orphans of the soul', restlessly relying on change and evolution, deafened by the noise which we produce in our futile modern cities.

Paul Valéry, pondering upon 'The Greatness and Decadence of Europe' after the onslaught of the First World War, said of Europe that it 'had all that was required to conquer and rule the rest of the world and to organise it for European ends. It failed in this task because of the lack of vision. Napoleon seems to have been the only one to have sensed what could happen and what might be attempted. He

[1] Erwin Schrödinger, *Nature and the Greeks*, Cambridge University Press, Cambridge 1957.

thought on the scale of the modern world, but was not understood and said so. The miserable Europeans preferred playing at Armagnacs and Burgundians to assuming throughout the globe the great part which the Romans had been able to assume and maintain for centuries in the world of their time. Their numbers and means were insignificant in comparison with ours, but they found more just and consistent ideas in a fowl's entrails than all our political sciences can muster between them.'[1] Before he died, he whispered: '*l'Europe est mort*'.

And yet, at the source of our civilisation, at the roots of our very being as Europeans, single voices are still heard singing of beauty and civility, of grace, of elegance, of perfection and refinement, of love and faith in the unchangeable eternal forces. And nourished by this powerful faith in man's dignity and God's universe, they have a genuine belief in the organic necessity and value of tradition. Far from being decadent or 'academic', they are vital and strong. They are carried by an unshakeable conviction of the importance of sophistication and of breeding, and they push aside any viewpoint dominated by our ever changing present, any Surrealist or Dadaist cynicism, any soulless and confused ideal of mechanisation, any chaos of disbelief, any materialism or the worship of speed, and they rigorously reject the idols set up some decades ago by those hypnotised by either cerebralism or by hysterical vitality only. They will not allow themselves to be seduced by the vulgarities of advertising techniques, by optical or perceptional phenomena only. They know how to work *sub specie aeternitatis*, they know of the secret of the conjunction of opposites, of the tragic quality of life and of the spiritual harmony achieved and achievable by human effort; they know the secret of Olympian humanism and of Christian tolerance which has been imbedded in their souls for millennia. The human quest is their task and their medium is art, the visible, the tangible, the natural, interpreted by the human mind and thus made accessible to the need of comprehending life without atomising and dissecting it only; the human need of acceptance and veneration. Marini, Manzù, Greco, what they have meant for our time, what they have achieved for us, how deep they have dug relying only on their inner voice, on their honesty, on their belonging – not on the findings of psychoanalysis or the depth-psychology of dissociated man – only the future will be able to disclose. Their work is the Swan Song of Europe. What will come after them in art will stand in the same relationship to their work as the new world-embracing outlook of industrialisation to the life of Europe unified in its spirit, the mother of it all, its first stage. What is happening in art around them in this decade will prove only the confusion of aims and means, disorientation caused by the shifting of the emphasis from man as the measure of all things in the sense of Protagoras, the Greek,[2] to the Universe, from man to matter, from cosmos to chaos, from quality to quantity, from the organic to the mechanic, from soul to brain. Arnold Toynbee said of this process:

'The prevailing tendency to abandon our artistic traditions is not the result of technical incompetence; it is the deliberate abandonment of a style which is losing its appeal to a rising generation because this generation is ceasing to cultivate its aesthetic sensibilities on the traditional Western lines. . . . Our abandonment of our traditional artistic technique is manifestly the consequence of some kind of spiritual breakdown in our Western civilisation and the cause of this breakdown evidently cannot be found in a phenomenon which is one of its results.'[3]

[1]*Reflections on the World Today*, Thames and Hudson, London, 1951.
[2]'Man is the measure of all things' (Protagoras c.481–411 BC, quoted by Plato in Theaetetus).
[3]Arnold Toynbee, *A Study of History*, Oxford University Press, 1946.

The Artist

Sicily is the largest and most stirring of the Mediterranean islands. Although it has not created a culture or a style of its own such as Crete, which acted as a stepping stone between the African continent and Greece, yet what it produced was a complex and fascinating pattern of styles and cultural influences. It was the crossroads of all Mediterranean civilisations. Embedded in a landscape which is varied and picturesque, combining pastoral-lyrical scenery with that of the most dramatic kind, lie the famous cities praised for their beauty by Pindar, surrounded by Homer's wine-dark sea, and here on this island we find myth and history interwoven to a degree as nowhere else. Greek imagination peopled it with legendary monsters and Homer's scenes from Ulysses, describing the hero's adventures with the Cyclops and the dangers of the treacherous Isthmus where Scylla and Charybdis threatened the lives of weary travellers, have their setting here. Colonised by the Greeks in some parts, and by the Phoenicians in others, Arian Greeks and Semitic Carthaginians lived side by side, tolerating and fighting each other in a land where peoples who had come earlier to this island had flourished: Homer's Sicanians of Iberian origin, later the Sicels of Latin origin and the Elymians of Indo-European origin. Always an attraction to other peoples, the Greek and Phoenician provinces of Sicily were subdued by Rome. Mohammedan Fatimides, the Guiscards from French Normandy, the German Hohenstaufen, rulers from Anjou, from Aragon, from Savoy, the Bourbons, the Hapsburgs, Napoleon, and even the English, governed Sicily at various times. Its history is the most bloody of all lands.[1] This land, which was so fertile that it induced Homer to write of its inhabitants: 'And we came to the land of the Cyclops . . . who trusting to the deathless gods plant not aught with hands neither plough: but behold, all these things spring for them in plenty, unsown and untilled, wheat and barley, and vines, which bear great clusters of the juice of the grape, and the rain of Zeus gives them increase';[2] this island, where Aeschylus is supposed to have died (in Gela), which was honoured by the visit of Plato, who tried here to realise his concept of an ideal and enlightened state; which inspired the poet Hesiod and whose history is related to us by Herodotus and Thucydides; this land, which because of its triangular shape was called by the Greeks Trinacria, whose geography was described to us for the first time by Strabon and Diodorus; this land, with its innumerable treasures of Greek, Roman, Arab and Spanish, Gothic, Renaissance and Baroque architecture and works of art, with its great wealth of information and the inspiration of its permanence, beauty and grandeur, is the homeland of Emilio Greco. A native of Catania, a town which, like Syracuse, has survived from antiquity, he is, as his name suggests, of Greek origin. Born in the nucleus of the Greek settlements on the north-west coast of the island – the colonisers were Dorians who first founded Naxos, and people from Naxos founded Catania, both in the eighth century BC – Greco is not only conscious of his heritage, he is a living link between the old Greek culture and its contemporary aspect. He is its direct continuation more than any living artist in Greece itself, which through five centuries of

[1] See the writings of Michele Amari (1886, 1930/39, 1949). Also: Fritz Schillmann, *Sizilien, Geschichte und Kultur Einer Insel*. Wien, Leipzig, Prague, 1935.

[2] *The Odyssey of Homer, Book IX*. Translated into English prose by E H Butcher.

Turkish occupation has changed completely in its racial disposition, with the consequent confusion in the traditional tenets of its heritage.

Catania and Syracuse among all the other Greek towns in Sicily, such as Megara or Segesta, Lipara or the beautiful Akraga, have left inextinguishable traces in his mind and memory, more so even than in later years did Rome, which became his residence and centre of activity after he left Sicily:

I run northward
to where no swallows fly
and no pines
glitter against the dark blue sky.
My body, only my body,
is on its way towards the north
is torn from you like a strip of flesh.
Stay with her there, dear soul:
at home be guardian to her heart.
Anguished this body only
travels northward
to where no swallows fly.[1]

Previously in Sicily he wrote:

Deeply embedded, all these stones
Are ripening, raised by the turf
In gentle wedges.
Around me the silence of ages
Touches my brow like a great bird winging.
Here I have lived for millennia:
And wisdom has been my companion
Throughout my long journey.[2]

'And wisdom has been my companion': the certainty of a valid tradition, the first impressions of grandeur made upon the soul of a sensitive youth, the reliance on his own feeling, this belonging to a past which is ever present, to the beauty of a landscape and man's ordering and organising mind, is that not wisdom? It is not mere knowledge, for knowledge without heart is dead; it is not erudite information for no cold process can leave such sentiments in the soul of a man who is predestined to become an artist. And as he carried Catania in his soul, so he built it up around him in his house and garden in Rome. The stones with which the paths are laid out there are of the same volcanic origin as those with which the streets of Catania are paved, originating from Etna, at whose feet Greco's town has defied its eruptions for centuries. In these walks, lined with pine trees, lemon and orange trees, with fragments of Greek, Roman, Renaissance, Rococo and Baroque sculptures, he feels at home. On one of the walls in his dining-room, there is a romantic late nineteenth-century painting by Michele Rapisardi from Catania, depicting Ophelia. A nostalgic figure, draped in a softly pleated garment, holding a flower in her hand, she wanders between trees and meadow plants. It made an unforgettable impact on the boy in his earliest youth when he saw a sketch of it in the local museum. At that time he read the poems of Rimbaud. One day, he found the original in the small shop of an antique dealer in Rome. Now it is permanently with him among many other much rarer paintings by master hands.

It was quite natural for a Sicilian artist to choose Rome among all the towns in Italy as the place of

[1] From *Emilio Greco, Poesie*, Collana Diretta Da Garibaldo Marussi, Edizioni d'Arte 'Fiumara', Milan, 1952. Translated by Eithne Wilkins.

[2] Translated by John Cairncross, in *By a Lonely Sea*. Hong Kong University Press, Oxford University Press, 1959. This poem 'Syracuse' is taken from *Emilio Greco, Poesie*.

his future activities. Rome was not only the organic centre of the country, the empress of all its cities, it was in many respects the climax of the Mediterranean culture. Here one cultural era had succeeded the other leaving the magnificent fragments of its existence, monuments to which mankind has made its pilgrimages since it was rediscovered as Europe's matrix. Here the history of European culture is made visible and true. Here are layer upon layer of cultural events manifest in stone and metal. The geology of European culture that is Rome, where Roman temples were changed into Christian churches and Renaissance palaces were built on old Roman bases or out of stones of the Colosseum and the Fora, where catacombs with their early Christian symbols and images were dug into the foundations of Imperial Roman walls, where the Gothic succeeded the early Romanesque, with its rare mosaics and ivory carvings, and the Baroque spread lavishly to demonstrate the splendour and power of the triumphant church over heresy and sectarianism. Here worked Fra Angelico, Bramante, Michelangelo, Raphael, here Bernini and Borromini added glory to greatness, here the spark of antiquity ignited the genius of Poussin, here Winckelmann retraced the classic spirit and started that avalanche of adulation which brought Goethe to Rome, Shelley and Byron. It is the town which inspired Stendhal to write his glorious *Promenades dans Rome*, the wittiest, the most intelligent and penetrating book ever written on a city, its history and its life. Florence is a precious gem, it was an arbiter of the *vita nuova*, but Rome is like a mother whose children have adorned her with the rarest gifts. Twice the centre of a world-wide reign, once in Roman, then in Papal times, it has conquered, governed and administered a world. *I could not live without Rome*, Greco once said to me. *Here the totality of Mediterranean culture has become a reality. Here the old humanist tradition is still a living fact. The all-embracing humanist idea, that is Rome for me. I can walk through Rome by day and by night. There are treasures everywhere, luminous traces of genius. When I stand on the Pincio and Rome stretches under me like a huge animal resting, breathing, I feel happy. I love the colonnades of St Peter's – it is Bernini's finest work. And his Fountain of the Four Rivers on the Piazza Navona – the whole world is in it. Look at the serpent, the horse, the lion and the flat fall of the water: a masterpiece. The triumphal arch of Titus is exquisite in its artistic economy. I love the Palazzo Farnese with its divine proportions and the Capitol, the centre of old Rome, in its unique beauty, with Marcus Aurelius, the complete and magnificent prototype of all equestrian figures in Europe. It was saved because he was thought to be Constantine. What an irony! Marcus Aurelius, the stoic, once said: 'Live constantly the highest life. This power is in a man's soul, if he is indifferent to what is indifferent'.*[1] *He had courage; he wrote his thoughts down in his tent, resting after the battles he fought for Rome; and he was sad because he knew about human nature.*

I love the colouring of the old Roman buildings, the ox-blood red of the terra di Pozzuoli, and the deep ochre. And in a letter he wrote to me: *There is no other place in the world which is so stimulating for work as Rome. Apart from all the traces of historic buildings and the echoes of remote and great civilisations like those of the Etruscan and Roman, it possesses a wonderful climate and colour (the green of the pines and the russet plaster of the houses) which excites my senses to the point of euphoria.*

In Santa Maria dell'Anima, the German church, I heard Bach for the first time. The Toccata and Fugue in D minor for organ. I was shattered. For me, sculpture is music and architecture. Calco matematico e cuore – *mathematical calculation and heart. This is true of Bach too.*

I was poor, very poor, when I first came to Rome. I had not more than 200 lire altogether. I ate nothing but sausage sandwiches, yet said to myself: I shall never leave Rome again. Before I had established myself in Rome, I designed patterns for textiles, and worked as a stone-mason as I had done before in Sicily. In Sicily, apart from funeral statues, I made portraits from photographs! They would not let me do this when anyone was still alive. Only when a person died then it became a necessity for them. On Sundays, I worked for myself. I also restored the interior of a church (Cattedrale di Carlentini, near Catania). In Rome, again I drew models for architects to earn some money. I was always hungry. They appreciated my

[1]Marcus Aurelius, *Meditations*, Book XI 16. Translated by A S L Farquharson.

work for I saw architecture as sculpture. It is only recently that I have been able to build myself a house according to my own ideas. I did it with a young architect. It was hell for him. I saw a line and said no; this is impossible, it must be changed. And so many parts had to be rebuilt – a protracted and costly procedure. The planning itself took two years. . . .

I love to be like a boy sometimes, to play about, to sing folk songs, Sicilian, Neapolitan. Because in my childhood I had to work too hard, I had too much worry. There is something sad in me, that is why I let go sometimes. I like freedom, my personal freedom and freedom from want. I have known hunger in Sicily, I know what I am talking about. We are free people, for us no formalism counts. When I was thirteen years old. I started to work. I got up at four o'clock in the morning to read,[1] at seven I went to work, pale and excited. My father was an artisan, an upholsterer. My mother gave birth to nine children. Only three sisters and a brother survived. My brother was killed in the war, somewhere in Africa. An aunt, the sister of my father, also lived with us – all in one room, in Catania. Those years in Catania, and the early years in Rome, were all lost for my art – I had to live. When I came to Rome, I had for the first time the opportunity of meeting people who understood what I strove for. I was confronted with the masterpieces of all art epochs. The evolution of an artist who lives in a big city like Rome is logical. In the museums, in the churches, in the palaces, all the artistic wealth is collected. We search for a personal style. Only maturity will bring it forth provided that one reaches it at all, that one gets mature enough and has the quality to achieve it.

The Greeks were artists by nature; they were always artists. But I have a great admiration for the Romans and their portraits too. Both were imperative for Europe. In fact, the Roman portraits are the most eminent human likenesses we know. And Greco, taking a book from one of the bookcases said: *Virgil was not entirely right in proclaiming: 'Others will make images of bronze and of metals so subtle that they seem to breathe. So I believe. And they will shape images out of stone with features so lifelike that they might speak in the assemblies. They will draw charts of all the thoroughfares of the Heavens and they will make known to all men the origins of the constellations of the stars. But thou, Roman, bethink thee that thou and thy Imperium have other things to care for. Thou art called upon to bear dominion over the nations. Those are the arts which have been allotted thee: To give laws for the maintenance of peace, to spare the humble and to strike down the proud'.[2]*

Emilio Greco's life as an artist started in his earliest childhood. Asked what is art, he will say: *I can reveal to you what it is* for me. *For me, it is the only necessity of life, to me it is like breathing, it is constitutional. When I was six years old, I felt happy when looking at pictures and drawings. I thought that I would like to do similar things. So I started to draw with a pencil on paper, with coal on walls, with everything on everything. I also worked in clay or mud which I found in the street. When we are small, our parents think that all this is a game. The main thing, however, is one's inherent constitution as an artist. I felt that this way was the only way I would like to live and work. When I was thirteen years old, I left school and went, as I have said, to a stone-mason. I worked for him in marble on crosses and funeral figures for cemeteries. In the night I modelled in clay, in the morning I studied art history. I read, when I was fourteen, books like Tolstoy's* War and Peace *or Flaubert's* Madame Bovary. *I read Dante and Leopardi. I knew whole Cantos by heart. I modelled by night from old plaster casts. During the day, when working on the cemetery sculptures, I learned the art of carving. My sisters have kept all the drawings which I made in those days.*

Training in a proper art school came much later; it was in Palermo, when Greco underwent his military service in the twentieth year of his life. In 1934, he asked for one month's leave and passed his examination at the Academy there. He was accepted with the maximum of votes and received his high school diploma (*licevo artistico*). He stayed in Palermo eighteen months, took part in competi-

---

[1] Greco read all the volumes of the cheap small size *Biblioteca Universale* of the Casa Editrice Sonsoguo in Milan.　　　[2] Aeneid VI.

tions, small exhibitions, and also made portraits. There was no art school in Catania. As well as drawing, he studied graphic techniques: lithography and lino engraving, no wood engraving. He knew how to work in clay, plaster and stone, in wax, in bronze. Even as a boy in Sicily he produced figures for churches, with one more than life size. This church was later destroyed, but the arch which sheltered his figure was saved. He often felt depressed about it. Emilio Greco does not like to speak about these early beginnings.

What is the philosophy, what are the thoughts about man and his universe, about life and living of this artist, who from a humble origin has become one of the leading sculptors of Italy, praised by the critics, honoured with gold medals and academic titles, congratulated in his success by royalty, presidents and popes?

My father, he said, *was a poor man and therefore a socialist. When I understood that Communism was a dictatorship, like Fascism, like Nazism, I did not want to have anything to do with it. The people in Russia are not free. I cannot believe in any dictatorship. I believe in man. I believe in the goodness of people. Even in war time, during a revolution, there is something, a tiny spot within the cruelty, in the centre of the cyclone where one can find signs of human goodness. I was moved by the diary of Anne Frank. I believe in freedom above all. The first law of life is freedom. I think that man must be respected as a personality. He is not a number, he is unique. He must have help from society, when he is young, to develop his gifts, and when he is old and cannot work any more, society has to help him again. With his life's work, he has given back to society tenfold, a hundredfold, what society has spent on him. This assistance of society must be dignified, not a charity. I also feel that if India is in a bad way now, or some of the South American states, that we are all guilty. The whole world is responsible. Violence is not a way out, only co-operation. We have a vision of a united Europe. This is a first step. I believe in this and the unity of the whole world.*

Eternal peace, as Immanuel Kant conceived it, is impossible. Such a concept does not count with the nature of man. Man, again, is not only instinct, man has a mind, he has the faculty of thinking. To curb the instinct and to find the balance, that is the task. There are certain limits in the condition of man dictated by political needs. America has proved it. It has achieved unity and with it greatness. On the plane of culture, of art, of humanism, there are no limits.

When we ask ourselves, what is life without love, the answer must be: nothing. Love is the first condition of life. Love is complete, love provides the natural equilibrium in man. Why violence? Where there is violence there is no balance. There is something else which is evil.

I am a Christian but not a church-goer. The Catholic Church is a vast organisation, often formal, sometimes stuffy. Jesus was a simple man, he did not like any pomp.

The Church, however, has done something great for the people of our time. It has called the best qualified artists to realize works for her purpose. As the finest example, I see at the moment Le Corbusier's La Chapelle de Ronchamp. This is modern religious architecture as Rouault's work is modern religious art, both of the first order.

I do not believe in God, I cannot. This makes me very unhappy. But I think nevertheless that God is necessary. If there were no God he ought to be invented by man. And he was. Man without God is defenceless against nature. Here is the limit which the human intelligence cannot overstep. We shall reach the moon, we shall reach the galaxies, but we cannot solve the mystery of Creation by cold science. Never. I cannot think that my body is composed of so and so many pounds of water and so and so many other ingredients – a bag of water. I cannot think like that. When I look at the beautiful body of a reclining woman, I look at it as a whole, I cannot think of it in terms of evolution. I cannot even imagine old age because it is physically ugly. Beauty is youth, blossoming, passing. But beauty must be restrained from inside – without the soul it is nothing.

Wherever you look around you, there is beauty. Beauty is everywhere. Beauty is in the petals of a flower, in its colour, in its harmony. The trunk of a tree, an animal, a fish, the sky, the sea, the mountains – they all are beautiful. But above all man, for he is the masterpiece, the loftiest expression of nature. As man we are nature in our bodies, we consist chemically of the same substance as can be found in the earth, in the sea, in a shoe. We are a part of nature. But if we can create we are more. Our work is not like the work of bees who collect pollen from blossom to blossom, and produce honey, that marvellous stuff. We take our impressions from nature, we take our impressions from love and suffering and we translate them into masterpieces for the benefit and enjoyment of man. We create. Not all people are artists. Of real artists there are very few in the world but just enough to produce a true sense of our life out of matter in the midst of brutality and primitivism.

Man has genius in many ways: it is clever to make glass or to construct a motor. A button, a needle are fine inventions. But there is no solution for our moral dilemma. The principal law of morality is what Christ taught – love one another. The categorical imperative is not a discovery of Kant's, it is Christ's. The defence of Mary Magdalene – 'he that is without sin among you, let him cast the first stone' – that is great. Jesus changed the short-sighted cruelty of people in the name of justice through love. I have loved very simple people. They were of low descent but had a pure heart. The most difficult thing in life is to have humility. When driving my car, I find day by day that people get more aggressive. To remain modest, that is great. I say to myself: Life produces suffering, my ambition produces suffering. Renounce like the Buddhist and you will have inner peace, Nirvāna. But is that right, is it not an escape from life, from responsibility? You must conquer your life every day with your work, with your example.

To grow old is dreadful, Greco once said to me. *Time is terrible. It creeps up slowly, but it reaches you in the end.* (A Greek thought even here.) *However, what I have learned in order to become human, through self-criticism, by way of living, I owe it to time. Every new moment of enthusiasm engenders my love of life. I do not strive after money, I do not need physical love – it is good in its time – but when I know that I can achieve something in the realm of the spirit, in my creative work, originality, that is my satisfaction.*

Youth and beauty are Greco's religion. He is more Greek than Christian. However, were not certain tenets of the Christian creed, certain motifs already present in Greek philosophy? *Sometimes I get depressed when I cannot catch the beauty of the moment. And I feel nervous without sun. My figures must stand in the sun. Do you know the secret of happiness? Never plan anything, let everything be a surprise to you: The light, the sun, the spring, a face . . . I love animals. We can always look at them to learn how to be true. And they are good. They kill only because they are hungry, not sadistically as we do.*

And as we find in Rodin's work the figure of the nude old woman, *La Belle Heaulmière*, the courtesan once radiant with youth and grace, now repulsive with age and decrepitude, once proud of her beauty, now filled with shame at her ugliness (Rodin said of the Greeks: 'They only permitted perfection of form and overlooked the truth that the expression of the most abject creature may be sublime.'), so we find in Greco's work one unique figure reminiscent of death: the *Dying Horse* (**13**) – a memory from the war, its destruction and its sufferings. He saw a dying horse on the beach in Catania.

Beauty is to Greco the key to life. Beauty creates love and love is the essence of Being. It penetrates all its realms, it gives all creatures the satisfaction of fulfilment. With this knowledge, with this belief in love and beauty, this pantheism of an ideal to be found everywhere in reality, he can proclaim – as Giordano Bruno did: 'Con questa filosofia l'anima mi s'aggrandisce e mi si magnifica l'intelletto – With this philosophy my soul grows and my mind is enriched.'

The one thing that counts in life is the heart, its feeling, emotion. It is the only link which binds people together. So he thinks, so he speaks and, unlike one of those modern Existentialist Bellerophons who feed sulkily and contemptuously upon their own nerves, far from the strivings of their contemporaries, his mind is open to man's happiness and life's uniqueness. He is opposed to the cynicism, brutalism and nihilism in modern art, his belief is in beauty, in meaningfulness and the miracle of Being. His works are the answers to our most perturbing inner problems. He lives in the good company of the great poets whose verses, whose rhythms, whose thoughts, accompany his own meditations, and he never works better than when listening to the music of the masters, to Monteverdi and Vivaldi, to Palestrina and Mozart, to Gregorian chants or the Mass of the Pope Marcello – to name but a few.

This then, is the artist, whose work we shall consider in these pages. As the child is father to the man, and as impressions from childhood are the most lasting and decisive, let us listen to what he himself has to tell us about this. We will learn from it how deeply he is indebted to the old folk culture of his homeland, how susceptible he was even then to the attractions of female beauty, its gentleness, its melancholy, its insistent grip upon him and how he learned about the obstinate and enduring presence of grief and suffering.

I was born . . . on October the 11th, 1913, in a house built beneath the road-level and I remember vaguely the enormous clusters of black grapes in the vine-trellis opposite it. Three years after my birth . . . we went to live in a small seventeenth-century house situated close to the University. Nearby, behind the Cathedral and the railway bridge, was the sea.

Below our house, there was a tavern with a courtyard. In front of it stood the Machiavelli Theatre (emblazoned with the names of Grasso and Angelo Musco) of which I remember the violent posters of famous fights between the paladins, painted with the intense blues and golden yellows that gave splendour to their cuirasses. Those were the dear puppets which I often drew on the pavement of our courtyard with any bits of chalk that I happened to find.

On the other side of the house, there were three windows with small goose-breasted galleries where I often sat with my legs dangling out, and blew into a stump of cane, sending down iridescent soap bubbles which vanished upon the black slabs of lava of our Cestai Street.

My father worked in the small room where I slept; and I remember the smell of the old dusty tow and the bunch of sorb-berries which hung from a pulley in the middle of the ceiling and which we let down every morning for a careful inspection of the ripe fruits.

When I looked out of the window over Cestai Street, I often saw Giovanni Grasso's mother, sitting in the gallery with her hands on her belly, a mild smile on her fat face.

I saw also, in the same street, other women showing themselves at the windows. They were women whom my mother warned me not to look at – sunu fimmini tinti *(they are painted women) she told me – and I recall those words which gave me a sense of disgust and curiosity without knowing the meaning of them. One day, without my parent's knowledge, I entered one of those houses to fetch a sparrow which had flown out of my hands. I went running into the dark corridor and up the staircase, summoning all my courage. I found a group of girls laughing on the landing and one of them gave me back the sparrow, looking with sweetness into my eyes. Her eyes were beautiful: I remember them for the tenderness and wonder that filled my soul whilst I expected to see who knows what bad faces.*

The First World War came. My father . . . was forced through lack of work, to seek employment with an information office for prisoners of war, and he earned one lira a day. I remembered that he came back home in the evening looking pale. My mother did needlework night and day and my sisters helped her as well, but with all this she did not succeed in stilling our hunger, and sometimes my aunt went out of the house to look for a five-lire loan to buy bread for me and for my poor brother who now rests in the Cirenaic desert, where maybe the wind has wiped away all traces of his burial place.

Then came the first elementary school and the fever of the drawing done by stealth on the pages of the copybook. My first lady-teacher was tall and dark, and I did not dare to ask her for permission to go to the toilet. In the same year, my eldest sister got married. I remember the taste of the traditional sweets, the procession of relatives from the house to the church and the grief mixed with jealousy that I felt when dear Ina left the paternal home.

I was still going to the elementary school when I used to spend whole hours in the afternoon in front of the shop of a barber, who had a beautiful apostle-like head.

He sat in his doorway and painted enlargements of the faces of dead people taken from card-size photographs. He worked for months on the canvas, keeping a magnifying lense fixed in his right eye.

I succeeded in persuading my parents to let me go to the barber-painter during the school holidays and for the first landscapes that I painted I used some colour tubes given me by my teacher, which had to be split open since there was nothing left to squeeze out of them.

The walls of the shop were covered with decorations after the De Carolis' fashion (at that time De Carolis were held in high esteem), and there were some women nudes with pointed breasts, and wisteria and poppies.

Poppy flowers also covered the cracks in the mirrors which were decorated enough already with excrement of flies. My employer once had the idea of keeping a small store of bicycles for hire, and he bought three half-rusty vehicles which were hardly able to stand up. Luckily enough, the tyres were full of air and he had the frames painted with those red and white spiral stripes which call to mind sweets of ropy sugar. The trouble was that the oil colour never dried on the frames, and the boys who came back from their strenuous runs had their seats striped like zebras and often refused to pay for the hire.

One of the most assiduous customers of the 'Art Saloon' was a sculptor, the author of several small funerary monuments copied from the catalogue of the cemetery of Milan. He worked very little because, as some malicious people said, the convenient dowry of his wife allowed him to do so.

He often struck the table of the 'Centrale' Café with his fists and said: 'I shall make Italy shake with my sculpture'. He was restless and showed newspaper clippings which spoke of him as 'the most powerful personality in Sicily'. Not very far from our sculptor lived a stone-cutter, who had invented a special putty which glued marble and then became as black as pitch.

One day, this stone-cutter took it into his head to make a model of a kneeling angel, and he built a trunk using a hemp bag soaked in plaster, to which he added the head, the hands, and the feet imprinted from nature, that is from his wife, and inserted them as joiners insert the legs of tables. The cemetery of Catania is populated with these winged ghosts of marble, and genistas blossom close to them on the black lava. Many angels with wreaths of chrysanthemums and tears of marble come from Carrara, made in sets.

I produced some of these too. . . . There it was that I learned rapidly to carve the marble and in the evening I stayed on until late to mould in clay fragments of classic works taken from plaster casts.

Sculpture and Drawings

(Heads and Figures)

You are kept safe now here behind this glass
like a jewel in its velvet box.
I caught this instant of your loveliness
to have you alone with me, companion to my thoughts.
It is as though you had gushed from the depth of the earth,
a well-spring;
as though the centuries had scarcely brushed
your cheeks to smooth their stony curves.
That other, she who posed for you
and gave me your eternal smile,
does not belong to me,
her soul impenetrable to my gaze,
even though I have kissed her marvellous lips.
But you are a created being all my own,
and here I keep you, in this studio,
in the silence of my love.

Conversation With My Sculpture[1]
Emilio Greco

No better definition of the work of Emilio Greco can be found than that contained in Rodin's judgement of Greek sculpture. Rodin, a *modeleur* like Greco and the greatest sculptor of the modern era, who attempted to build up his contemporary work on the basis of the European tradition, to fulfil in the spirit of our time all that the heritage of the Greek, Roman and Gothic art meant to us as Europeans, said: 'The Greeks were simply scholars, their art was pure geometry. The Beauty conceived by the Greeks was the order dreamed of by intelligence; she only appealed to the cultivated mind, she disdained the humble; she had no tenderness for the broken; she did not know that in every heart there is a ray of heaven. – She was tyrannous to all who were not capable of high thought.' And yet: 'Sculpture was never more radiant than when it was inspired by this order. It was because that calm beauty could find entire expression in the security of transparent marbles; it was because there was perfect accord between the thought and the matter that it animated. . . . No artist will ever surpass Phidias – for progress exists in the world, but not in art. The greatest of sculptors, who appeared at a time when the whole human dream could blossom in the pediment of a temple, will remain for ever without an equal.'

'Without doubt, the Greeks with their powerful, logical minds instinctively accentuated the essential. They accentuated the dominant traits of the human type.'

'It is madness to believe that they despised the flesh. Among no other people has the beauty of the

[1]From *Poesie*, translated by Eithne Wilkins.

human body excited a more sensuous tenderness. A transport of ecstasy seems to hover over all the forms that they modelled. Thus the difference is explainable which separates the false academic ideal and Greek Art.'[1]

My history begins in Rome
Emilio Greco

The first significant sculpture in Greco's work, one of the last made in Sicily just before the Second World War broke out, is the head of a man. He calls it *Little Man*, (**4**). It shows a stylistic affiliation with Etruscan sculpture. What the artist is preoccupied with here and in all his later heads and portraits is the synthesis of the character of the model, its psychology, and the sculptured form. In this early case, the psychological interest predominates. It is in fact a drawing on the surface of the clay. The realistic details are accentuated, the eyes, the moustache, the beard, the wrinkles. Greco is in search of the human truth. What is man? Here, quite instinctively, by way of the details, the 'little' man is characterised in all his narrowness, his friendliness, his helplessness. Nothing transcends this limitation. What an enormous step forward in the purely sculptural sense is the head of the *Wrestler*, 1947 (**10**). In its small version, the volume dominates, indicated by the firmness of the body, the limbs and the ball-like head. It is pure architecture. In the *Large Wrestler*, 1947/48 (**8**), the psychological element comes to the fore once more but it is subordinated to the sculptural form. Greco represented this fat man, who, combining strength, kindness and naivety, performed before a street audience, as a character somewhat akin to Charles Laughton, although slightly ridiculous in his histrionic realities. Here the amalgam of the Etruscan, the old Roman and the modern is already successful. It may be that the inspiration derived from Marini's work helped towards its realisation. Both have the same roots, struggle with the same problems in the face of an age old tradition. An analogous work to the *Wrestler* is *The Singer*, 1947 (**11**), again a motif from the street, a style similar in conception. Another step in the same year and the year after, and we encounter the *Head of a Man*. The first, a lyrical, the other, an epical characterisation (**5/6**); in both heads, expression and form in balance, the two inter-penetrated, a complete sculptural statement. One cannot help feeling that the head of 1948 even contains an element of self-portraiture; it has a certain likeness with the young artist, it depicts his poetic attitude to life. By contrast, all his other male heads are those of mature, calculating, active men, making firm decisions, represented with the pitiless realism of the old Romans and with a grain of irony, even of satire, in the spirit of Aretino or Cecco Angiolieri. The head, round like a full moon, composed of concave and convex forms, the smile in the one face, the restraint in the other, the eyes of both shut. This is the case also in the *Head of a Man* from 1951 (**7**). There are two of them. It is as if the artist did not wish to break through the closed form with a look which would destroy it. All these heads represent types. They are all alive, though reminiscent of old models. The most outstanding seems to be the head of 1951, from the Olivetti Collection, with its strange, forlorn and mysterious smile, produced with sensitive scratches on the surface and slightly displaced planes. The number of male heads and figures is limited in Greco's work and if we add the early *Head of Man* (1944), the *Portrait of a Man* (1947), *Sitting Man*, produced many years afterwards in 1962, (**9**), *Head of a Man* 1965, (**1**) and another *Head of a Man* (1968) as well as a few portrait drawings, we have accounted for all. In 1968 Greco produced a head of 'Christ' for the Pope's secretary Monsignore Macchi. In its powerful and realistic rendering it makes one think of certain of Meunier's heads of workers. In Greco's reliefs, particularly in the late monumental ones, there are male figures and heads as part of a given theme. Also, in commissioned works such as medals, coins and stamp designs male heads occur.

Greco is predominantly the sculptor of the female face and shape. To represent womanhood, that is his calling and his task. The grace, the delight, the beauty, even the power of womanhood. Neither

---

[1] *Auguste Rodin, Art.* By Paul Gsell, Hodder & Stoughton, London 1912. Translated by Romilly Fedden.

Marini nor Manzù can compete with him in this respect. Marini's female bronzes are mature Pomonas, while Manzù's dancers give only one particular although significant aspect of female aesthetics and psychology. Greco however, is completely absorbed in womanhood as if the myth of the Great Mother,[1] the Lady of Elche,[2] the White Goddess,[3] had come alive in him again. He represents youth, virtue and sensuality; he even knows how to make the dignity of a matron attractive. But he never allows himself to appear frivolous or carnal. And, in this respect, his influence may prove of importance for the unleashed sexualism of our times. He loves Demeter as much as her daughter, Proserpina,[4] Chloe as much as Lycaenion,[5] and so he has become the sculptor of female maturity and of girlhood as well. Wherever he strikes, a note resounds against the mentality which surrounds us; a true echo of its age. For the Greeks, the mature woman was the ideal type, Venus more than any other goddess. Our civilisation will be defined as one which gave preference to youth, or rather to teenage youth. Nevertheless it is not the sex baby which attracts Greco, the product of the screen and the glossy magazine, but youth, the fast fading blossom and its nostalgia, the symbol of life stretching out as an unfulfilled dream before us at the beginning of our way. Greco has produced in his sculptures and drawings of female youth an equivalent to the presentation by great European writers of the young man with his melancholy, the enigma of love in his veins and sorrow in his heart and eyes: Flaubert's own image as a young man in *L'Education Sentimentale* and in *Novembre*, written 'pour niaiser et fantastiquer', Goethe's *Werther*, Alain Fournier's *Le Grand Meaulnes*, Jacobson's *Nils Lyhne*', the shy hero of Dostoyevsky's *White Nights*, Hamsun's Johan Nagel in *Mysteries*, Thomas Mann's *Tonio Kröger*. It is young womanhood as Sappho could describe it when in Antiquity she spoke of the 'honey-voiced virgins':

> *Now she shines among Lydian women as*
> *when the red-fingered moon*
> *rises after sunset, erasing*
> *stars around her, and pouring light equally*
> *across the salt sea*
> *and over densely flowered fields.*[6]

And Proust in our time! Who could not speak of this chain of portraits, sculptures and drawings made by Greco of girls and young women, from 1949 onwards, as having been produced *A L'ombre des Jeune Filles en Fleurs* ? 'Were they not noble and calm models of human beauty that I beheld there, outlined against the sea, like statues exposed to sunlight upon a Grecian shore?'[7]

The representations of women and girls do not appear in Greco's work in the same style as the male portraits and figures. The Greek and Gothic impact are felt immediately. The Greek in *Girl's Head* (1947), and in *Figure* (1948); the Gothic in *The Cyclist* of 1947 (**44**). We have already indicated previously the link between both – the smile which makes sisters of the Kore in Chiton and Peplos of the Acropolis Museum, the Crouching Aphrodite from Rhodes, Queen Uta in the Dome of Naumburg, the Sabina Poppaea of one of the masters of the École de Fontainebleau, and the charming Bathers of Renoir. This smile which blossomed in the women of Cretan wall paintings, in Da Vinci's Mona Lisa, in Munch's Madonna, on the faces of Japanese ladies in the prints of Utamaro, is the smile of the Sphinx. Was it not Kokoschka who once said of Greco: 'He is the Utamaro of modern

[1] Erich Neumann, *The Great Mother*. An Analysis of the Archetype, Routledge & Kegan Paul, London, 1955.

[2] André Malraux, *Les Voix du Silence*, Gallimard, nrf., Paris, 1951.

[3] Robert Graves, *The White Goddess*, Faber & Faber, London, 1948.

[4] Proserpina (Persephone, Kore) married to Hades (Pluto), God of the Underworld.

[5] From Longus' *Story of Daphnis and Chloe*. Translated by Paul Turner, the Penguin Classics, 1956.

[6] Sappho. *Lyrics in the Original Greek with Translations* by Willis Barnstone. Doubleday Anchor Books, New York, 1965.

[7] Marcel Proust, *Seascape with Frieze of Girls*. Vol. II of *Within a Budding Grove*, Chatto & Windus, London 1924.

sculpture, a rare artist with a wonderful sense of form and a tender sensuality. Modigliani seems insipid by comparison. He is lacking in artistic intelligence.' And Henry Moore, the prophet of anti-perfectionism, the antagonist of Greek beauty, had to confess from the heart of his titanic-barbaric rebellion: 'Greco is not only sensual and elegant. He has a feeling for beauty, and also a natural sense, a gift for form and volume – a rare combination.'

One could characterise Greco's young woman in the words used by Chateaubriand when speaking of Mme Recamier: 'Complete harmony dwells in every line of her face which radiates essential gentleness, nobility and goodwill. The very qualities that distinguish her beauty shine forth also in her nature itself. And yet there is in her also a dainty impishness, coupled with a romantic imagination which, seemingly at variance with her normal air of complete serenity, lends her a quite special charm. Often she uses passionate words, but even while she is uttering them her face never loses its expression of shy innocence. . . . Under the spell of such a rare fusion of opposites, one feels that she possesses a twofold power of attraction – that of the virgin and that of the beloved. Like Venus, she seduces, and like the Muse, she inspires. In a rapture of love, a man might fall at her feet, were he not overmastered by a feeling of reverence for her.'[1]

The *Girl's Head* of 1947 and the head of the *Figure* of 1948, do not show that penetrating search for the psychological as we experienced it in *Little Man*. The genus Woman exercises in them its magic directly. The inspiration may have its source in the *Dying Niobe* (44 BC) from the Terme Museum in Rome. Greco – who in his feeling comes near the Ionic style, on whose mind the Aphaea temple of Aegina, the work of the Gothic Italian masters: Giovanni Pisano, Benedetto da Maiano, Arnolfo di Cambio, Tino di Camaino, Benedetto Antelami, made lasting impressions, true impressions because experienced by a congenial temperament – has also much in common with the aristocratic refinement of the French Rococo, with the sensuality of Indian temple sculptures. And that the Baroque, with its representations of the Earthly and the Heavenly Love, had much to offer an artist who lived in a city dominated by this style, is obvious. We find the Baroque torsion and its oval form in his work (*The Skater* II, 1959, [46] and most of the female portraits) as well as the undulating plant line of Art Nouveau, with its roots in Chinese and Japanese Art. And we find also a strong abstract element in all his mature work, i.e. from the moment it became a personal expression of his humanism and his craftsmanship. When he speaks of *calco matematico*, of geometry, and even architecture in sculpture, he means that abstract element which he proclaims every good work of art must contain, together with rhythm – the music of it all. Concerning abstraction, in the contemporary sense of the negation of all figurative and recognisable features, he accepts it as a polemic fact only. *I do not think that abstraction is useless, on the contrary. Any true artist can accept the positive, constructive part of it and repudiate all that is sterile, arbitrary expression. What has been realised up to date by the abstractionists, however, cannot be called vital.* Greco even speaks of its trend as an 'academic' one which remains chained to a scheme without any poetic possibilities. *What is more abstract than a human body?* he once exclaimed. *The poetic experience! Phantasy! Everything comes from phantasy! What was the outcome of the battle of Troy? Not science – it was a feast of phantasy: Homer's Iliad and Odyssey. Our age has not enough of it. Modern man has no wings, no idealism. He can fly from Rome to London, but not from where he is to his dream, his ideal. And it is only this which embellishes life, gives it a new dimension. Few people appreciate nowadays the beauty of a figure, very few. Everything is mechanistic, utilitarian. I belong to another age, I am not a man of this century. I am a man of many ages: Egypt, Ancient Greece, Rome, Baroque. I am not only Rococo, as some people think. Rococo is too extrovert, too sweet, superficial. My work is not only sensuous. I like to construct, to apply lines strictly. The Neapolitans are superficial, they live in a Verdi atmosphere. People from Sicily and Calabria are deeply rooted in their sentiments. They love or hate, there is no middle way. Nature has provided them*

[1] Edouard Herriot, *Madame Recamier et ses amis*. Gallimard, nrf., Paris 1934.

with a melancholy feeling, it is inherent in the race. And with a strong voice, he started to declaim Leopardi's 'Infinito'.

> *This lonely hill was always dear to me,*
> *And this hedgerow that hides so large a part*
> *Of the far sky-line from my view.*
> *Sitting and gazing*
> *I fashion in my mind what lies beyond –*
> *Unearthly silences, and endless space,*
> *And very deepest quiet; until almost*
> *My heart becomes afraid. And when I hear*
> *The wind come blustering among the trees*
> *I set that voice against this infinite silence:*
> *And then I call to mind Eternity,*
> *The ages that are dead, and the living present*
> *And all noise of it. And thus it is*
> *In that immensity my thought is drowned:*
> *And sweet to me the foundering in that sea.*[1]

Leopardi is very near to Emilio Greco's heart. Greco is not perturbed by the strong melancholy undertones, which might seem opposite to his own cheerful temperament – this, however, only seemingly. In the rich stratas of his nature, Greco combines both the tragic and the hedonistic sense of life. What he admires in Leopardi is his great mastery, the genius of his language, and it is for this that he is as dear to him as Dante, Petrarch and Boccaccio.

The *Figure* of 1948 expresses an emotion, an inner movement, a movement of the soul; *The Cyclist* of 1947, a physical movement. Similarly, also *The Skater* I (1947, destroyed by the artist) and *The Skater II* (1959), and some of the Bathers and Dancers (VI, **27**-8, **34**-**41**), the standing figure of *Chiara* (1959) and several designs on medals. In *The Cyclist*, and even more in *The Skater*, movement as the main motive unfolds the rhythm of the body. It inspires the artist, suggesting endless possibilities. It is a dance whereby the body is likened to a whipping top. There is nothing more musical than a body in movement. The movement in Greco's *Cyclist* and *Skater* is arrested, but in the sculptural sense living, giving the essence of life which is movement; not a dead mechanical movement, a stroboscopic fraction of a second torn out of its organic flow, dissected, atomised, senseless, as we see it in Duchamp's *Nude Descending A Staircase*. Myron's *Discobolus* has a wonderful rhythm and so has Rodin's *Le Jongleur*. There is rhythm and movement in every vital sculpture or it would not be a work of art. Hence also the Baroque S-Line and the Baroque torsion in all these figures of Greco's, for the Baroque was the style of violent movement, Expressionist in its character and exciting. The opposite principle in Greco's sculptural research is realised in *The Ox*, 1948 (**12**), the beast in a closed rounded shape, a wholeness like a gigantic netsuke, like Brancusi's egg-shaped form, Egyptian. We may remember here what Michelangelo once said, when contemplating some antique torso; that the thing to do was to roll a figure downhill over rocks; what remained of the figure after this ordeal was sculptural. There are several examples of a similar kind of sculpture throughout the ages. The nearest in time to Greco's is *The Bull* of Arturo Martini of 1941. Greco was walking near Rome. He was sketching and saw the ox, white, monumental, one of those of the gracious long-horned race which we enjoy amidst the Italian countryside. He tried to approach him,

[1] The Infinite. In: *Poems from Giacomo Leopardi.* Translated by John Heath-Stubbs. John Lehmann, London, 1946.

but the animal rose. When the artist stopped, the ox stopped too and then lay down again, so Greco drew him from afar and experienced him as a piece of marble enclosed in its own form.

Another significant trend we can notice in the two female representations, the *Figure* of 1948 which was repeated in a new version in 1950 (**47**) and *The Cyclist*, in comparison with the male figures. In his representations of female figures, Greco proceeds from the type, the genus, to the individual. The individual is represented for the first time in the *Portrait Bust* of 1949, with its faint smile. This bust already shows all the elements of stylisation so typical of Greco's concept, which seems sometimes about to approach a certain mannerism but never ends in a mannerist trend, such as we find it in Fazzini's or Mascherini's work. Contemplate this row of female faces, drawn and sculpted, which like a string of pearls, adorn the work of this unique and sensitive artist. Has not his own country discovered the prototype of the ideal beloved in Dante's Beatrice, in his Paolo and Francesca, (later to become the first theme to be drawn by Greco in a series of lithographs, for *La Commedia di Dante Alighieri*) and in Petrarch's immortal poems to Laura? Dividing in Greco's work the faces of the young and the mature woman, we shall find an apotheosis of youth, of beauty, and the eternal womanly (in the sense of Goethe, the creator of another Beatrice type: Gretchen in Faust, as Ibsen was of Solvejg in Peer Gynt), unsurpassed in the history of sculpture. What individuals they are! There is the *Head of a Woman*, a pen drawing of 1949 (**113**) already a fully-fledged Greco, with its seductive smile and a certain aggressive sharpness which makes one think of the approaching dangers so blatantly exposed in Baudelaire's Vampire:

> '*Toi qui comme un coup de couteau*
> *Dans mon coeur plaintif est entrée. . . .*'[1],

or in Edvard Munch's narrow-lipped beauties. The earlier drawings are not yet personal, though masterly. Here, however, with its flowing lines and its pointed characterisation, the personal style is achieved. Many of the early drawings, as some later ones too, are pure line drawings, melodious, vibrating, flowing or again angular, economic in their means and always alive. Then again the need of a more plastic rendering was felt, the three-dimensionality achieved by means of shading and cross-hatching, which became, by about 1954, intensified to such an extent as to produce the wished-for effect through the denseness of the cross-hatching, without the use of any outline at all. This style is brought to a climax in the large scale drawings of 1963–66, the apotheosis of youth par excellence. Only the head in profile, *December 1967*, tells of a crisis which the artist went through in his private life.

The smile again of the *Portrait Bust* of 1949 is gentle, though the tension expressed in the nostrils and the curve of the mouth is evocative of a woman rather than of an angel. Venus is dormant in every Chloe.

The way to Greco's representations of mature woman is opened by *Fiorella*, 1949 (**17**). She is the Lycaenion in Longus' book, the first novel of Europe. Compare the faces of both the *Seated Figure* of 1949 (**16**) and the *Large Seated Figure* of 1951 (**IV**). Could they be more different as representations of human character and destiny? Each one has her own story and each could form the content of a book. From the sitting position of the female shapes, let us proceed to the lying position. The *Large Nude* of 1952 (**62**) is a work of rare excellency. It could add beauty and lustre to Versailles with its delicacy of expression and grace of movement, and, placed in Fontainebleau, would express its essence. *Lia* (1956) is the modern Sphinx, the riddle of womanhood, as subtle as the famous Greek marble sculpture: *The Birth of Aphrodite from the Sea*. Now in the Terme Museum in Rome, it was originally carved about 460 BC in one of the Greek colonies of Sicily, Greco's homeland. *Sibilla* (1951) expresses by its very name that mixture of wisdom and seduction, the mother and lover component of womanhood, whereas in *La Peruviana* (1954) and in *Aretusa*, 1954 (**60**), a demonic quality

[1] Charles Baudelaire, *Les Fleurs du Mal*, G Crès, Paris, 1925.

25

finds its form. Greco, however, never attempts to achieve a dramatic effect (or its opposite, the comic, the grotesque), as we know it, from the heads of the Medusa or the tragic masks of Greek Antiquity. His is a lyrical and epic talent, not a dramatic one. The Roman inspired *Portrait*, 1952 (**15**) is a matron who knows about life and can manage it, a reigning figure, an empress. *Nanda* (1954) is the young woman in full bloom, beautiful, with the classical proportions which attracted the artist personally. She became his wife, bore him a daughter, Antonella, and inspired with her face and body many a work of his. To her, he addressed his poem Sunrise:

Catania is still asleep on the sea-weeds
that lap its volcanic rocks
the sky does not perceive this face:
the war, still awaiting us, the war.
If you hold out your hand, – sister
I will make for you white statues.[1]

In the same year, the portrait of *Anna* (**43**) is made, the young woman who, from then on, dominated the artist's vision and whose figure determined his most important series of sculptures – the Bathers. In 1962, Greco made a portrait of her, her arms raised – one of his finest pieces (**III**). In the *Sleeping Nude* (1951), with its Japanese traits, Greco reached another peak of his achievement. The sculptural and rhythmical arrangement of body and limbs in the round is as natural as water flows and the rush moves in the wind.[2] The manner in which the arms frame the face, and the limbs fold up and are at rest – and then the hands! Greco, when producing the portrait *Pamela II*, 1962 (head, shoulders and right hand, **61**), said: *The artist has a relationship to his ideal, to his dream. And he has a relationship to his model. He works in order to reach his dream. All that he is doing in achieving it is invention. The human body is all invention. The artist reaches his aim by applying geometry beside and beyond the likeness, the expression. Everything in a sculpture must be vital and conceived in the round. A sculpture – figure or portrait – consists of a continuous sequence of profiles. Every line must be alive and correct. Every single sculpture is built up of innumerable planes, lines, details which are asymmetrical. This conveys movement, life. Nothing must remain dead. Take a Gothic figure! It is composed with a frontal view. If you look at it from another side, it collapses. I believe in the Greek and Egyptian idea. A figure is like a column. Your eye wanders around it without interruption, musically. I often work to music. One of my best figures was made when I listened to Vivaldi's Concerto,* The Four Seasons. *I speak of my Grande Bagnante I (Large Bather I).*

The *Sleeping Nude* of 1951 leads directly to the *Crouching Figure* of 1956 (**51**) which is most probably the finest closed sculpture produced by the artist and again one of his greatest achievements. The Japanese, those highly civilised and refined connoisseurs, the masters of tea and sophistication in everyday life (Zen) enthused about it as they did about the *Grande Bagnanate I* (which now adorns one of the squares in Tokyo). There are two versions: one from 1956 and the second from 1961 respectively, (*Large Crouching Figure*, **57**) – the first more captivating and small (height 26 in.), the second (height 51 in.) calm and great and mature in its majesty. It may prove one day to have been the finest figure produced in this century, serene and pure and classical as it is in its appearance and rendering. An ideal concept of a modern woman as convincing as any Greek Venus.

What a range of expressions, of moods, of charm and dignity, can we find in all these faces. *The Woman of Trieste*, 1954   (**20**) does she not remind us of Lucia from *I Promessi Sposi*?[3] In the softness

[1] Alba, in: *Poesie*, 1952.
[2] I am reluctant to speak of angles and planes, concavities and convexities, of volumes thrusting forward and receding, for I believe that this is, above all, a highly spontaneous work, the result of a happy moment of creativeness.

[3] Alessandro Manzoni, *I Promessi Sposi*, A Signorelli, Rome, 1953.

of its execution, it makes one think of Medardo Rosso. And the *Parthenope*, 1957 (**24**) in cement reminds one of a character taken from a Greek tragedy, Parthenope being a figure of Greek myth, as surely as *Iphigenia* in Greco's work, a bust similar to Parthenope but in bronze, 1961 (**65**).[1]

If the face is that part of the human being which determines it most distinctly as an individual – and Greco often accentuates it in his drawings through shading and cross-hatching, distinguishing it thus from the rest which often remains indicated by ingenious outlines only – then the hands are no less important. Those hands in Greco's works, those playful, caressing, clasping hands, hands pressed into the flesh like fossils into stone or growing out into space like branches! That pattern of

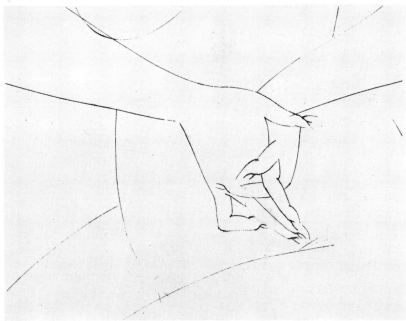

Study of Hands: Detail of Figure, 1952.

Study of Hands: Lady combing her Hair, 1961.

[1] Parthenope, the daughter of Stymphalus, is a tragic figure of Greek mythology. Iphigenia was the daughter of Agamemnon, destined to be sacrificed by her father to Artemis. Greco particularly loves this name.

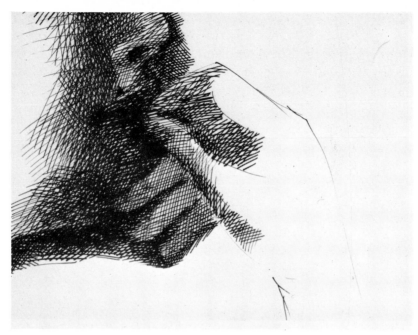

Above: Study of Hands: Meditation, 1963.

Below: Study of Hands, 1949.

wrist and back and fingers bent or stretched out, fingers relaxed or prohibiting, fingers apart and fingers tightly closed, gripping and relaxing fingers. It is a microcosm of forms and expressiveness, often used in a decorative manner. And as decorative too and expressive is the use Greco makes of the style of hair.

Pamela I, 1954 (**14**) is like a poem of Nordic beauty, a saga of enchantment and inspiration. The artist then wrote:

> *You are standing before me white.*
> *Can my hands give you life*
> *for all the love they feel?*
> *No vicissitudes of life*
> *or even the erasing touch of the wind*
> *will change your face,*
> *the smile of stone.*
> *And poets will carry through the centuries*
> *an echo of your beauty,*
> *perhaps remembrance will remain of you.*
>
> *When your caressing hands*
> *Rest on your children's heads,*
> *This light, Pamela,*
> *This southern light,*
> *Will rest in the blue of your gaze*
> *As on some far-off lake-side,*
> *And nothing will be gentler than your eyes:*
> *Pamela.*[1]

The Woman of Massa, 1955 (**22**), with outstretched forefinger, is strongly cut into the clay and anticipates the determined spatula work in the portrait *Pamela II*, 1964 (**61**) and in the portrait of *Marisa Ciardiello* (1958), a pupil of Greco's from the Academy in Naples, and one of his finest. This powerful tendency in style, the strong and summary characterisation of a personality, found its full expression in the artist's hitherto latest portraits, in *Patricia, Michela, Maria Baldassare, Michaela,* (all 1967) and finally in *Eiko*, 1968, (VIII).

Might not *Malgari Onnis*, 1953 (**19**) be taken from one of the stories of Francis Jammes, which all bear girls' names as titles, names filled with romantic scents and murmurings like heavy dreams: Clara, Almaide, the little Rose. It would be of no avail to describe the faces of all the Bagnantes, the Degas-like face of *Chiara*, 1959, (**26**) the stern features of the *Olympian Victory*, the Torch-Bearer, produced for the Olympiade in Rome in 1960, (**48**, v). Let us conclude this review with *Luna*, 1961, (**66**), the bud-like girl, Eve before the Fall, a lovable primary image, gay and carefree, curious and thoughtful on the verge of entering life, of leaving the paradise of youth behind, innocence. No power is as strong as Eros, no nuclear fission can destroy life.

> *I think I have found a new synthesis*
> *of the human form in the Mediterranean*
> *tradition.*

Emilio Greco

---

[1] Translated by Eithne Wilkins.

With the *Grande Bagnante I*, 1956 (**29**), a new phase begins in Greco's work. What is a Bagnante? Renoir, Degas and Bonnard drew and painted women in their most intimate occupation: taking a bath. Greco shows the female body exposed to air and sunshine, breathing in the glittering atmosphere which is absolute freedom, the very *joie de vivre*, an image of happiness and inner peace. He shows it slender, oscillating slowly in the health-giving rays like a flower moving in the wind, a blossom opening under the caressing touch of the warm summer rain; a body feeling its perfect roundness in the refreshing element of the water, opening up and closing again like a ripe fruit. What the *Man on Horseback* is for Marini and the *Cardinal* for Manzù, the *Bagnante* is for Greco – a theme with variations. Endless possibilities arise before his sculptor's eye. He has found himself in complete fulfilment as the poet of the female body. He himself considers the *Bagnante I* to be one of his most important works.[1] *I shall make new statues, find new movements expressing the same idea*, he exclaimed one day. *That is me, I feel it. When, some time ago, I made new portraits, new figures, I found there was no progress. But this was novel as well as perfect. This statue stands like a tree. India understood how to make its sculptures grow as nature does. There is air around them, the space is dominated by the figures. The other large Bagnantes are like dancers, demonstrating the harmony of movement, mood and spirit. This is the goal! There is no development in the figures themselves, the lines are the same as before, but the idea is to produce a multiplicity of movements and, seen from the sculptural point of view, to achieve the ideal of body architecture: Like the vaults of a bridge – limbs and body are composed.*

There are seven versions hitherto of the Grande Bagnante theme (VI) and ten small versions. There are also small versions of the Seated and Crouching Figures in Greco's work. A number of the Bathers were produced first as small figures and later as large ones, but some remained only in their small versions. It is the movements of the arms and legs and the torsion and beauty of the body which distinguishes them. The crowning achievement of these series of works, the quintessence and the synthesis of his entire art and experience are contained, according to the artist himself, in the *Grande Bagnante VII* and the *Large Crouching Figure II* (both 1968).

Of his *Bagnante I*, Greco also said that, with this figure, a new research began for him into the rhythm of the human body. Greco was at the time inspired by the music of Orpheus and Eurydice by Monteverdi. Anna Padovan posed for it and thus she entered the story of his art, after having taken part in his life for some time. She became his second wife in 1969. To Greco, she represents security and the firm foundation of his existence. He portrayed her in the gesture of holding up a heavy plait of hair with her right hand. In the carriage of her head and shoulders, her personal pride is expressed. The body moves as elegantly as if it were a Gothic figure. It is not sweet but round. The form is pure, the outline is closed within an elipse. *I will die but Anna will remain*, he once murmured thoughtfully in front of this work. The large standing figures of *Chiara* (1959) and the *Olympian Victory* (1960) are of the same range but have different aesthetic functions.

In his book *Les Cathédrales de France*,[2] Rodin said: 'The great tree has its part in the creation of the monument'. And analysing the question of 'Rodin and Some Archetypes of Space', A M Hammacher wrote: 'One of the preliminary studies for the Balzac figure is in reality the scarcely human figure of a tree rising out of the earth, – the figure of a willow split asunder, in which Balzac, animal-like and primitively human, conceals himself like the spirit of the tree.'[3]

Greco, when producing his standing female figures, felt his way in the same direction: Figure – Tree – Column.

---

[1] The other works of the same importance are, in his opinion, *The Monument of Pinocchio*, and *The Doors for Orvieto Cathedral*.

[2] Librairie Armand Colin, Paris, 1921.
[3] In: JP Hodin – *European Critic*, Cory, Adams & Mackay, London, 1965.

Monumental Tasks

I believe in Man
Emilio Greco

With his aesthetic credo well defined, Greco embarked on works which emphasised the ethical side of life and art. The possibility was given to him in monumental tasks which could unfold his still dormant faculties to work on a large scale with complex subject matters. The first one was the *Monument to Pinocchio*, the puppet which became a human being. It was erected in Collodi, the home town of Carlo Lorenzini, who had adopted the pseudonym of Carlo Collodi. The book has a high educational value, the invention of the figure of Pinocchio was a stroke of genius, the work a literary masterpiece of world fame. In 1953, a competition was promoted in which 179 sculptors and architects took part. 80 maquettes were submitted. Greco won the nation-wide competition. This was of the same significance for his reputation as was the Italian national prize of sculpture awarded to him at the XXVIII Biennale at Venice, 1956, for his figure of the *Grande Bagnante I*. His position as a sculptor was established. Another climax had to be reached, however, in the design and composition of monumental reliefs which made him a sculptor of international repute. We will deal with it in the section on the bronze doors for Orvieto Cathedral and the monument for Pope John XXIII in St Peter's in the Vatican. It took three years to accomplish the *Monument to Pinocchio* the puppet, from the first sketches and the maquette, via the plaster model, to the finished bronze statue which stands 16 ft. 4 in. high and is placed in the playground of the Pinocchio Park in Collodi (**76**).

From a base which has the shape of a tree trunk, a fine example of an abstract constructive conception – sufficient in itself, as it were, for an abstractionist who deliberately refrains from the human element – grows the figure of Pinocchio, or rather the story in its crowning climax, represented by the fairy, the guardian angel or good spirit who has fulfilled her task, and the puppet itself, surmounted by the fairy bird. What is depicted is the transformation or the transfiguration of a puppet into a human being with a soul, responsibility and lofty aims. This commission was of the utmost importance for Greco, for here he could engage his talent for the first time in the free display of his phantasy and the combination of several figures.

The story of Pinocchio stimulated Greco's imagination in inventing the forms and figures of a composition which for him was a translation of a human idea into sculptural language. Pinocchio was the first work where Greco suddenly felt what the freedom of invention, what phantasy meant. It was a conquest. He said to me: *In general, our life as artists in our modern civilisation passes by in the utmost solitude and isolation. I believe sincerely that every work ought to be stimulated by a theme or by an occasion which in itself carries the chance of application to our own life. I do not believe in any work produced in the studios without such a scope, without any purpose. L'art pour l'art is a dead formula.*

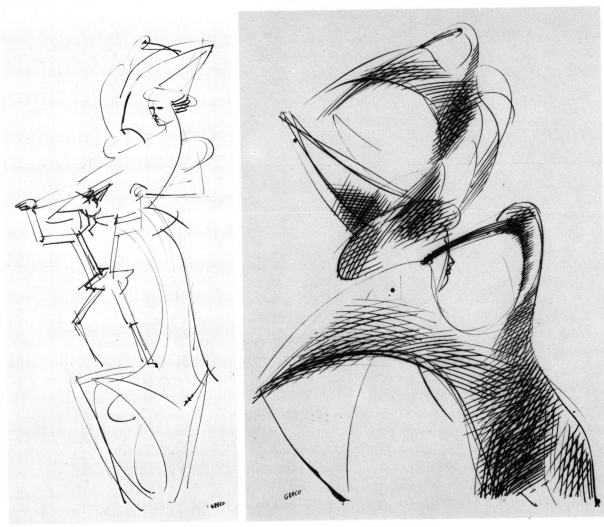

Study of Pinocchio, 1953. Study of Pinocchio, 1953.

We must revive our civilisation with the feeling for the necessity of rendering an account of political, moral, or religious content, i.e. with a belief in our mission to represent the meaning and the conditions of life, be it in religious, political or moral terms. It was with the Monument to Pinocchio, *for the first time, that the opportunity was given to me to shape a story with a significant moral scope, for children. This moral scope is personified in the guidance by the fairy. The transformation of a shapeless, nasty child which, through the guidance of a fairy, becomes a human being – that is a great theme. The wooden puppet becomes a man.* Greco represented the story at that very moment of action when the puppet is transformed. The meeting between the caring and loving fairy and the puppet was conceived as a dance, a rhythm in the phantastic atmosphere of a wood where anything supernatural always could happen. What actually happened is real, is reality and, at the same time, a miracle which we all experience, the humanisation of our existence. The fairy's dress changes gradually into the trunk of an olive tree (we are reminded of the mythological theme of Daphne, so popular among sculptors still in the Baroque age).

The puppet is represented on this base of the monument in a pirouette movement, holding the fairy's hand and glancing happily into her face. At last he has understood the lesson. The fairy looks at him like a mother, a sister, and a large bird concludes the spiral composition, beating the air as a symbol of liberation. It is thus that Greco conceived the idea of the narrative, translating it into sculptural terms, building an imaginary tree trunk with its rhythm of outer and inner forms, its fullness and its hollowed out volume – a tower of inner achievement. The work on this, his first monumental task, was a strenuous one, but, as in the Pinocchio story itself, a sudden inspiration solved the basic sculptural problem. In a letter of the 17th September, 1955, the artist wrote to me: *Every evening, I used to read to my daughter, Antonella, the story of Pinocchio of which she was particularly fond. When the competition for the monument was announced I had no idea as to how I would be able to translate into plastic form a conception so abstract as that of the puppet, and for many months I thought hopelessly of various secondary figures as* Leitmotifs, *without it occurring to me that the fairy herself would suggest the best solution.*

It was Antonella who, by asking me insistently for explanations of the significance of the fairy, gave me unwittingly the key to the best solution for the composition. After that, she followed closely the progress of the work, understanding perfectly, as she did, all the characters in the story.

This confession explains fully the great appeal which the artist was able to transmit to the motherly figure of the fairy. There are few female faces in Greco's work which radiate such a determined gentleness as this and the movement of her arms and hands holding those of the puppet suggest a mild firmness, the rhythm of love. Children play now in the tree trunk base of this sculpture which symbolises their youthful pains and struggles, their early defeats and victories.

This idea of an upward movement in man's psyche, expressed compositionally in a screw-like torsion, is also present in the design for a monument of 1956, which Greco undertook in co-operation with the architects Vincenzo, Lucio and Fausto Passarelli, in a competition for the building of the headquarters of the United Nations in New York, and a similar one for the headquarters of the Christian Democratic Party in Rome. They were, however, not executed. The composition itself reminds one of the designs of 'The Mountain of Men' – completely unknown in Italy – made by Edvard Munch for the main wall of the murals for Oslo University, again unexecuted, and replaced by the picture of the rising sun. As here, the theme was *Elevazione dell' Anima* or *Elevazione Humana – The Elevation of the Soul of Man.*

In October 1955, a competition was announced for a monument to the founder of the Olivetti factories, the engineer Camillo Olivetti. Greco did not take part, but as no decision could be reached on the basis of the submitted models, a second limited competition took place and fifteen artists were invited to suggest ideas, including Greco. Greco accepted the challenge and co-operated with a young architect Silvana Panzarasa who, later on, also built his own house and studio in Rome. Together, they worked out a maquette for the monument which won the prize (30th March, 1956). Among the judges was Marino Marini. On the 29th September, 1957, the monument was unveiled (**69**). It is composed of a column-like construction in bronze placed on a stone base in the midst of an oval basin with a flat waterfall behind it, in front of which, and asymmetrically placed to the right of the great structure, a large plaque with a bronze relief of the Olivetti portrait stands out. It is joined to a horizontal bar which, thrusting through the waterfall, is fixed on the rock behind it. The column consists of enlarged models of typewriter keys, ingeniously composed, a perfect construction. Again, as in the tree trunk of the Monument of Pinocchio before, and later on in the two side-doors of Orvieto Cathedral, which show only a rhythmic pattern of squares irregularly applied and produced by a hammer beaten into the clay, thus serving as a background to the figurative elements, two hovering angels of terrestrial, superterrestrial beauty, the artist seems to have demonstrated the futility of any geometric or ungeometric abstraction as a sufficient expression for human content.

Before we approach the climax of Emilio Greco's work hitherto, the doors for Orvieto Cathedral and the monument to Pope John XXIII in St Peter's in the Vatican, let us consider first the reliefs which he produced during the early years of his career. It must be said, however, that the reason for these early works having been produced in terracotta only, including that fascinating small figurine of an old woman, *The Fortune Teller*, a perfect work of art, from 1944, which did honour to his artistic faculties as well as having saved the life of his family from starvation during the war,[1] was purely economical. He had no money for casting them in bronze.

The first relief in his work represents a *Country Dance* (1945), clumsy heavy figures not particularly rhythmical and composed as if on a horizontal strip, with a reclining woman in the forefront to accentuate depth. Yet impersonal as this flat relief was, it represents nevertheless a certain technical adroitness in its summary treatment, achieving more of a painterly than a sculptural effect. Contours and volumes are not strictly defined. The strength of Greco's mature sculpture lies in its melodious, exact and refined outline and its masterly balance of rhythmical volumes. There is a *Deposition*, a relief produced in the American Red Cross establishment in Rome, (1944), of a similar quality. Strangely enough a late relief in bronze depicting *Christ Falling for the Third Time on His Way to Golgotha* in the Church of Santa Maria di Monte Santo in the Piazza del Popolo (1964) shows the same type of *va presto* work, fast and sketchy and even impersonal.

In the *Samaritan* of 1950 (**90**), which was made on the occasion of the 'Anno Santo', this early stage is overcome. Here we see Greco's whole subtlety already in the characterisation of the figures, the expression of their faces, the sophisticated way in which he alternates flatness and height in his reliefs, his strength in the rendering of the human content as well as the masterly composition, drawing, as any Italian artist does, on the ever present and inexhaustible treasury of traditional forms and images both painted and sculpted.

The work on the bronze doors for Orvieto Cathedral was started in 1950 and lasted for more than five years, during which time some other major works were conceived. Let us discuss them here: there are, first and foremost, the five high reliefs for a new church near Florence, *La Chiesa dell' Autostrada del Sole, S. Giovanni Battista a Campi Bisenzio* (IX, X), a complex architectural construction of great originality created by Guido Lambertini, designed by Giovanni Michelucci, with Saverio Giacomini advising on the subject matter and the realisation of the artistic decoration of the church. Many artists have worked on the proposed themes and have produced stained glass windows, sculptures in metal, tapestries, mosaics and wall paintings. Emilio Greco was commissioned to design five reliefs representing the deeds and fates of the patron Saints of the towns of Milan, Piacenza, Parma, Reggio Emilia, and Modena through which the Autostrada leads southwards.[2] The reliefs are composed for the five parallel side walls of the East Narthex, where a strong light from the left streams through a high window. The artist, taking this light into his calculations, produced relief figures as if cut out, to stand isolated and in a strong silhouette against the stone background. They are reminiscent of mediaeval representations of the stations of the Cross. The Saints and the scenes of their life chosen for this purpose are:

Saint Ambrogio, patron saint of Milan

[1]The following story is connected with it: Greco had suffered very much from the absurdity and cruelty of war. He not only had wasted eighteen months of his life in military service during 1934/35; when the war broke out, he was called up and lost six more years for his work. The irony of fate decreed that Greco, the great admirer of the Ancient Greeks, his ancestors, should spend this time as a soldier in Albania, near the Greek frontier, in bad conditions, freezing and starving, an enemy to himself, so to speak. All this folly and the destruction, made him desperate. When the opportunity came and Greco was back in Sicily, he deserted from the Fascist army, hiding in the forest to await the approach of the Americans who had invaded the island. With them, he entered Rome, earning his living by drawing portraits and producing medals of soldiers and officers in the American Red Cross establishment. In the care of the Americans, he no longer needed to starve, and, as he lived on his portraits, so there was an elderly Italian woman who lived on her art of reading the fate of the soldiers from their palms. Greco made a small sculpture of her sitting in an easy chair, on which he worked unusually long. Did he do it for the pure love of art? The guards at the entrance smiled at the emaciated Italian artist who every evening carried his unfinished sculpture home from the American Red Cross. But there was a secret to this unfinished work. The sculpture was hollow. Greco filled it each day with American cigarettes which he received for his work apart from the money that was paid to him, and as he was not allowed to take them out, he placed them safely within the sculpture, producing a new bottom of soft clay every evening and thus carrying away this most precious currency for which anything on the black market could be exchanged.

[2]The sculptor Venanzo Crocetti produced the reliefs representing the remaining towns: Bologna, Florenz, Rome, Frosinone, Caserta and Naples.

(teaches the singing of his hymns to the faithful imprisoned with him by the imperial forces in the Basilica of Porzia).

Saint Giustina, patron saint of Piacenza
(her decapitation in the presence of the Emperor Maximilian).

Saint Ilario, patron saint of Parma
(his disciple, Martin of Tours, brings to him the missal given to him by an angel, so that the saint could celebrate Mass).

Saints Crisanto and Daria, patron saints of Reggio Emilia
(martyrdom of the wedded pair, on the floor of a Roman amphitheatre).

Saint Geminiano, patron saint of Modena
(exorcism of the daughter of the Emperor Gioviano).

Greco chose for his task a style partially Baroque yet again severely Romanesque, in a rather rough staccato technique for the purpose of arresting the light and producing deep shadows with figures sometimes breaking through the relief composition and becoming semi-round sculptures. The impact on churchgoers passing by on the right of the bronze screens to reach the entrance of the nave is violent, intended to produce an immediate and quick effect.

Before the doors of Orvieto were cast, Greco was approached by the Chapter of the Basilica of St Nicola in Bari to produce designs for the three large doors of the church. He made drawings for this purpose in 1963, in which the history of the Saint who gave his name to the English Santa Claus and to St Nicholas on the Continent is depicted. They represented the Birth of the Saint; the Miracle of the Three Poor Girls for whom St Nicola provided the dowry so that they could marry (it was an apple of gold); the Miracle of the Three Boys Condemned to Death, who were saved from execution by the timely arrival of St Nicola; the Miracle of the Ship Wreck, and finally the Transport of the Mortal Remains of the Saint by Sailors to the St Nicola Basilica in Bari. The doors have not yet been produced.

A further commission was for a bronze relief for the corridor of the passenger ship *Michelangelo*, representing *The Return of Ulysses*, 1964 (**91**), an appropriate theme for people travelling on the sea. In its sculptural treatment, it stands between the reliefs of the church at Campi Bisenzio and those of the Orvieto doors. The scene depicted is one combining that of the old servant-maid Euriclea, who recognises Ulysses' wound when washing the feet of the beggar, and the dog who first knew the presence of his master – this dog appears also in the Orvieto doors and, later on, in the Monument of Pope John XXIII – in the background Penelope. The relief is composed diagonally, the point where the two diagonals meet is also psychologically the most important point: the knee of Ulysses touched by the head of the servant-maid bound by silence, the dog barking and standing with his paws on the maid's legs, and Penelope are in one diagonal, the direction of the mass of Ulysses' body, his gaze and the face of the maid in the other diagonal.

The importance given to the three new bronze doors for Orvieto Cathedral (**92–103**) has been stressed by the artist several times. The task was enormous, the responsibility great. Two years were spent in intensive work. *I sometimes worked for twenty hours without a break – I was as if in a trance. The Doors of Orvieto – that is the most important event in my life as an artist. Through it, I came into creative relationship with one of the finest examples of church architecture (Gothic period) in Italy. It was indeed a challenge when the Office of the Opera del Duomo Di Orvieto approached me with the request to consider the commission. I trembled with fear and doubt, the idea terrified me. To add something of value to a building of such perfection weighed heavily on my mind. I asked for time to decide and, meanwhile, I went every day for months from Rome to Orvieto and back, to think, to look – and to hesitate again. I sat opposite the magnificent building, wondering how I could have been so foolish as to believe that I could produce something that could stand up to the grand and subtle work of Andrea Pisano*

Study of Centre Door of Orvieto Cathedral, 1961.

Study of Centre Door of Orvieto Cathedral, 1961.

and Orcagna: to the exquisite rosette, the sculptures, the precious and rich reliefs in marble adorning the triple façade; something that could take its modest place on the magnificent front of this building without destroying its purity and grandeur. When the themes were proposed to me – they were connected with some episodes from the Crusades, or alternatively with the legend of the miracle of the Bolsena Wine that turned into blood (a priest celebrating Mass and not believing in the divinity of the wine at the moment when he raised the chalice above his head, was converted by the miraculous fact of the wine overflowing from the vessel on to the altar, staining it with blood), I remained emotionally untouched. I felt I could not produce anything of artistic and human value connected with such themes. But when, finally, the Corporal Works of Mercy, those capital commands of human behaviour were suggested to me, I accepted immediately because I felt strongly that this theme was congenial to my belief. It is an eternal theme, perpetually occurring, not only a historical one, a human theme, not only one connected with the church. Pope John XXIII really visited the inmates of a prison in Rome and that impressed me tremendously because of its truly Christian gesture. I saw the Pope several times speaking to the people, good as he was, and mild and strong: 'My dear sons, it is late, the moon rises, go with the Lord and tell your children that you have seen the Pope'. It was so simple, so true. And then the letters which he wrote to his relatives! They were very poor and humble people, like himself. The Italians really loved him.

When I pondered on the sculptural side of the problem, I felt strongly that the making of any low relief was technically comparable to that of an incised medal. What I was concerned with also was the vibration to be created when the light struck the surface of the doors. I thought I achieved it through the rhythmical pattern produced by the hammer which left mosaic-like traces in the clay. The modelling of the figures in the various scenes has the touch of a personal 'Cubism'. It is a question of forms composed in several movements in one single representation, producing dynamic perspectives. These figures can be seen differently from different points or angles.

In a letter of the 27th December 1963, the artist wrote to me: *There were never any bronze doors at Orvieto.*[1] *The ones in existence are of wood and only provisional. For almost a century, the Opera del*

---

[1] Owing to the controversy between the Ecclesiastical Authority and the *Opera del Duomo* on the one hand and the *Consiglio Superiore Delle Belle Arti* on the other, Emilio Greco's bronze doors were not fixed in position until 11 August 1970. The Consiglio was opposed to the installation of the doors because they were opposed in principle to the installation of modern works of art in historical buildings. During the six years of the controversy the doors were placed in the cathedral.

To Feed the Hungry, 1963. Detail, Study of Centre Door of Orvieto Cathedral. Drawing in Indian Ink, 28 × 20 in. *Museum of the Opera del Duomo, Orvieto.*

To Give Drink to the Thirsty, 1962. Detail, Study of Centre Door of Orvieto Cathedral. Drawing in Indian Ink, 28 × 20 in. *Museum of the Opera del Duomo, Orvieto.*

Duomo di Orvieto, a body which is responsible for the conservation and maintenance of the splendid edifice of the Cathedral, sponsored various competitions in this connection, but they all proved fruitless, owing to the mediocrity of the works presented for consideration. When, in 1959, I was approached, with the eventuality in mind of my executing this work, I recognised the enormous moral importance of such a commission. . . .

In the episodes To Comfort The Imprisoned *and* To Clothe The Naked, *I have wished to represent historical events, like those of the visit to the prisoners made by Pope John XXIII, and of Saint Martin, who divided his cloak to share it with the poor.*[1]

It is clear that the problem of including my work within the framework of an historic building which is pre-eminently Gothic gave me some anxious thought: Finally, however, I sought to express myself in a modern idiom, naturally not ignoring tradition, but indeed making it my foremost consideration. I did not wish to impose any limits, certainly not archaeological ones, on my spontaneity, whilst not in any way yielding to my pride. What I hoped for was to impose a rule of the intelligence which should lead to a cohesion of the work with its preceding antiquity whilst remaining independent of it. In the central door, which measures 23 ft 6 in. in height by 6 ft 9 in. in width, the divisions are in accordance with the modular disposition of the facade and are related with sensitive precision to its height and lateral scoring. The side doors, which measure 14 ft 6 in. in height by 6 ft 9 in. in width, are modelled with a subtly calculated surface vibrato from which emerge two angles in the form of great handles.

In September 1964, Greco spoke to me at length about this work: *I saw all the important doors in Italy, to discover how the great artists solved such a task. I saw the Romanesque church of San Zeno in Verona, with its low reliefs by Nicolo and Guglielmo of the 12th century, and the superb bronze panels of the doorway; the doors of S. Ranieri in the Dome at Pisa, the two bronze panels of which are the work of Bonanno Pisano (1180). I studied once more and again, with particular zest, the South door, by Andrea Pisano (1336), with its frame by Vittorio Ghiberti (1403–28) and the North door by the same Ghiberti, of the Baptistry of the Cathedral in Florence, the wooden door of Santa Sabina in Rome, with its 18 carved panels. It dates from the first half of the 5th century. Further, the fine bronze door of Ravello*

[1] The other Works of Mercy are: *To Feed The Hungry, To Give Drink To The Thirsty; To Harbour The Homeless; To Visit The Sick; To Bury The Dead.*

To Clothe the Naked, 1962. Detail, Study of Centre Door of Orvieto Cathedral.

To Clothe the Naked, 1961.

To Clothe the Naked, 1961. Detail, Study of Centre Door of Orvieto Cathedral.

To Clothe the Naked, 1963. Detail, Study of Centre Door of Orvieto Cathedral.

To Harbour the Homeless, 1962. Detail, Study of Centre Door of Orvieto Cathedral.

Cathedral by Barisano da Trani, and the doors by the same artist in the Cathedral by Trani in Apulia (both made in 1179); then the wonderfully sculptured bronze doors of the Cathedral in Benevento from the 13th century, unfortunately badly damaged in the last war, and the bronze door of the Basilica of Monreale, the most beautiful Norman church in Sicily, by Bonanno da Pisa, dated 1186.

When my work was finished, I visited it often to compare it in my mind with the great works I had studied and admired on my journeys to and fro throughout Italy. And he added: *I often feel sad and despondent when looking at my old sculptures. But here it has happened for the first time in my life that a finished work produces in me, whenever I see it again, the feeling of satisfaction. I have worked so intensively on it that I found myself with my right arm practically crippled. For months, I was unable to move it at all. I suffered from an inflammation of the nerves which rendered me unable to sculpt.*

So Emilio Greco drew. He made countless large size drawings of young girls – thus not only sparing his overstrained muscles and joints, but relaxing from the work which had made such heavy demands on him. Never before has Greco achieved such outstanding results. His sensibility, technical skill and his taste are here at their best.

Let us return to the doors and state a few important data related to me by Dr Arch Torquato Terracina, who is in charge of the *Opera Del Duomo di Orvieto*.

1 The invitation to Greco to prepare a sketch for the doors was made in May 1959. He accepted it in principle, without, however, giving a precise undertaking, reserving to himself the right of further confirmation when he had succeeded in making a work to his own satisfaction and approved by a commission of experts appointed to deal with the project.

2 Agreement was reached between the sculptor, the Ecclesiastical Authority and the *Opera del Duomo* that the themes should be *The Corporal Works of Mercy*, as being relevant to the work of the Church, complementary to the iconography of the Cathedral and the one most congenial to the personality of the artist.

3 Greco signed the contract in December 1962, after the approval of the advisory commission on the project of the sketch and of a part of the left panel of the central door which had already, in actual fact, been modelled (To Bury The Dead, and To Comfort The Imprisoned).

4 The doors, cast in Pistoia in the Michelucci foundry arrived at Orvieto on the 4th August, 1964.

39

It is to the credit of Monsignore Giovanni Fallani, president of the Pontifical Commission for Sacred Art in Rome, and to Dr Torquato Terracina, architect of the Opera del Duomo in Orvieto, Professor Enzo Carli, Professor Fortunato Bellonzi, and many others that they have not only supported the artist in his struggle but that they have also fought for the idea of the incorporation of modern works of high quality in existing historical buildings.

The style of Greco's door for Orvieto is the mature and personal expression of a sculptor at the height of his technical and artistic development. It can be compared with outstanding modern works such as the doors by Giacomo Manzù for Salzburg and for St Peter's in Rome, or even with old famous works such as the doors of the Baptistry of Florence Cathedral.

Greco's style approaches here the Quattrocento conception rather than that of the reliefs made for the S. Giovanni Battista church. Only the angels on the two side-doors have a greater affinity with the Baroque. The pattern of these side doors spreads over the middle door and creates a unified rhythm of vibration. In the left hand upper field, the host of angels, as if falling from the heavens to be the first to aid suffering humanity, carry grapes for the thirsty and sheaves of wheat for the hungry; on the right-hand side, they assist men in their sorrowful duties of burying their dead. To express this compassion, two of the angels hold hands. What a daring composition is the wing of one angel standing at right angles to another angel, flying as it were out of the frame of this scene, thus closing the composition and leading the eye downwards to the central group of mourners. The kneeling figure in the foreground is as if in revolt against death, echoing the artist's own dread of this unchangeable final fact. And the faces! Expressive in their simplified forms, masterpieces of an artist's shorthand, the result of decades of work and consciousness of style. Here and there, these faces pressed into the background appear heightened only in the figures who are the main actors of the scenes depicted. There is such a subtlety of movement and rhythm in the relief representing the episode of The Visiting of the Sick, such a power in its refinement, such a masterly handling of the forms that one can say without hesitation that barely any modern work can match it in excellence.

In one respect Emilio Greco has also created in these doors a personal monument to himself. With the humour of the great artists of the past, he has portrayed himself and Anna Padovan (both in profile) in the relief depicting The Visiting of the Sick (XI), his daughter Antonella (en face) in the relief depicting The Clothing of the Naked, and his friend the sculptor, Giacomo Manzù (three-quarter face, in the same relief), his friend the art historian Fortunato Bellonzi (the first profile on the left in the relief depicting The Visiting of the Sick), and even his dog Bobby.

The back of the door is adorned with three coats of arms: The one of the *Opera Del Duomo*, the other of the Bishop, the third of the Dome Chapter. They are both decorative elements, and the confirmation of acceptance. The following inscription in Latin is added:

'AENEA HUIUS PORTAE VALVAS CAELATIS OPERIBUS EXORNATAS SEPTIMO REVOLUENTE SAECULO MIRACULO EUCHARISTICO APUD VOLSINIOS LITTERISQUE APOSTOLICIS "TRANSITURUS" MIRABILITER FECIT AEMILIUS GRECO SCULPTOR URBEVETANA BASILICAE DECORE FELICITER AUCTO ANNO   MCMLXIV.'

Pope Paul VI, who visited Orvieto for the inauguration of the doors, expressed his appreciation of the work. Soon afterwards, he gave the artist proofs of his sympathy. After having previously considered from him a design for a series of stamps for the Vatican post commemorating the centenary of the foundation of the Red Cross (the inscription reads: *Samaritanus Misericordia Motus Est*, (XII), he asked him finally to produce the over life-size monument of the 'good' Pope, Pope John XXIII, for St Peter's in the Vatican. Emilio Greco always had a great respect and love for this dignitary who initiated a veritable change in the spirit and outlook of the church. He also appreciated the fact that the good Pope, as a man of very humble origins risen to the heights of his office, had a heart for the people. He defended the truly Christian content of the creed. All this made Greco well suited to produce this work requested from him, a monumental bronze relief. The space reserved for it was in the second chapel on the left of the main entrance, not far from a most exquisite work by Antonio del Pollajuolo, the bronze monument of Innocent VIII (15th Century) and the elegant monument to the Stuarts by Antonio Canova, the master of Neo-Classicism (1817).

Again the artist was faced with a dilemma. Here he had to produce for the leading Basilica of Christendom, a work in the vicinity not only of Camaino's famous sitting statue of St Peter, of Michelangelo's Pietá, but also of the pompous Baroque medallions in coloured marble which, carried by *putti*, surrounded the very space where his relief had to be placed. The result of endless meditations was his determination to be and to remain himself. His first sketches show the Pope en face, in robes and mitre, surrounded by cardinals. Later he portrayed him in profile, his mitre on his head, dressed in his robes and kneeling, his hands clasped in prayer. Finally he is standing, robes and mitre unchanged, his right hand raised, blessing the sick. His face is that of a strong personality, not sweet as many liked to see him. For Pope John XXIII was a great man, determined in his universal love of mankind – he saw in all men, coloured or white, his brethren – kind, faithful to friends and his family, ambitious, industrious, imbued with courage and patience, a lover of children, with the sense for the mission, dignity and calling of women, joyous and enduring, suffering, perpetually giving thanks for the gifts of life, religious, but not blinded by dogma and simple, even primitive, in certain of his reactions. He had outbursts of rage and hot temper and again he was full of humour. There are countless anecdotes concerning him. His deeds have determined the face of the Church in a time of danger and spiritual crises. *The Journal of the Soul*,[1] a kind of inner biography, speaks of his personality as intensely as his deeds give proof of his greatness. Greco represented him in the midst of these deeds (**105**, XIII). There are the Corporal Works of Mercy again, as in the doors of Orvieto: In front of the Pope the mother and the sick child; the blind and paralytic man with crutches; a standing, a sitting (it is the artist's daughter Antonella) and a kneeling woman sufferer, and as a dramatic background, the prisoners behind bars. The head nearest to the Pope, represents the author of this book. Again, a host of angels storm downwards in a Baroque vision – the turbulent upper part of the composition balances the quieter lower part. One angel approaching the Pope carries an olive branch, for the Pope published the encyclical letter *Pacem in Terris* – Peace on Earth. He also initiated the second Ecumenical Council for the reform of the Church and peace between the churches. In Greco's composition, this is represented by three heads of cardinals – a Chinese, a Negro and a White – in mitres close together, two of them facing each other, as if whispering. At one time during the work it was doubtful whether the dog in the maquette for the relief would be acceptable for St Peter's. The artist then intended to replace it, if circumstances had so commanded, by the outstretched leg of a sitting blind man. There was, however, no need for any change.

The relief in parts high (as in the group of angels and the Pope himself) in parts low (the left side of the composition with human figures), the play of concavities and convexities in which the light is caught vividly, some details left sketchy, others again worked out minutely, the folds, the rhythm and pattern created by the spatula and other decorative elements, all this leaves a strong and dynamic impression which is dominated by the calm and majestic figure of the good Pope, standing there like a column in a heavy sea. The monument is 23 ft high, 26 ft 6 in. including the red-brown porphyry base for which the artist designed the name: JOANNES PP.XXIII in the lettering of the early Christians. The width is 9 ft and the depth 2 ft.

In its style this commemorative relief of Pope John XXIII has a direct link with the Orvieto doors, and this not only because some of the same motifs appear in both works, but also because it is born of

[1] Geoffrey Chapman, London, 1965 – Giovanni XXIII, *Il Giornale dell' Anima*, Rome, 1964.

the same spirit. Already in 1962, Greco had produced a drawing of Pope John XXIII in profile, his Mitre on his head (not the Tiara), his right hand raised to bless. (**154**)

This relief is more than an accomplished work, it is a personal confession in the context of a true humanism. The monument was consecrated and unveiled on the 28th June 1967 in an intimate ceremony by the Pope who honoured the artist in the presence of eighty-six cardinals and the entire *Corps Diplomatique*. During the ceremony Pope Paul VI presented the artist with Pope John XXIII's walking stick made of hardwood from the Philippine Islands, inlaid with mother of pearl, the handle adorned with the coat of arms in enamelled silver, further the magnificent opus 'I Vangeli Secondo Matteo, Marco, Luca, Giovanni' (Editiones Officinae Bodoni, Verona, 1963) with the dedication 'A Emilio Greco con la nostra benedizione – Paulus PP. VI – 28.VI.1967', and to his daughter Antonella a golden chain with a medallion of the Madonna made by Manfrini. Already previously the Pope had shown his personal sympathy in sending the artist the two volumes of 'La Sacra Bibbia', illustrated by Rembrandt (Garzanti, Rome, 1964) with the dedication: 'A Emilio Greco nel natale di Cristo auguri e benedizione – Paulus PP. VI – 24-XII-1965'.

Between 1958 and 1960, Greco produced fifteen lithographs to illustrate scenes from Dante's *Divina Commedia*. Thirteen of them are contained in the three large volumes produced by Aldo Martello.[1] Many other artists have contributed to the same work. Two of Greco's drawings depict scenes from the Inferno: Paulo and Francesca, Inf. V. terz. 43: and Thaïs, Inf. XVIII terz. 44. Six scenes from Purgatory: Pia dei Tolomei, Purg. V. terz. 45; The Annunciation, Purg. X, terz. 15; the dramatic scene with smoke and fire (sepia) from Purg. XVI, terz. 8; Mathelda Picking Flowers, Purg. XXIII terz. 14; Beatrice on the Carriage with Angels and Virtues, Purg. XXX, terz. 45; the picture of The Church as A Whore and The Giant (France) Sinning With Her (sepia), Purg. XXXIII, terz. 15. Five scenes from Paradise: Dante with Apollo and Minerva, Par. II, terz. 3; The Repudiation of the White Man and The Rehabilitation of the Black Man, Par. XIX, terz. 37; David with his Lyre, Par. XX, terz. 14; St John and Christ, Par. XXV, terz. 38; (**155**) and finally the Appearance of the Lady to Eve, Par. XXXII, terz. 2. All of them are drawn in black, with the exception of two in sepia. Emilio Greco now cherishes the idea of one day illustrating the entire Divine Comedy.[2]

In 1967–8 the artist produced forty-two drawings to illustrate Ovid's *Ars Amatoria* (Die Liebeskunst, Edition Propyläen, Berlin, 1969) (**160/1**). Single illustrations of the artist occur in various publications, for instance in *Dante*, A cura di Umberto Parricchi, (De Luca Editore, Rome, 1965), in the 'Boccaccio' edition of the publishers Mondadori (I Giganti La Nuova Biblioteca Per Tutti, Rome), in *Epitaph*, Karl Amadeus Hartmann, (Munich, 1966), and in *La Sacra Bibbia* (The Holy Bible) Illustrata Nell' Arte Italiana, (Editrice Italiana di Cultura, Rome, 1967).

The artist also produced various illustrations for book covers: 1. *Josephine Carson*, Incalza La Mia Verde Età (Drives My Green Age), Romanzo, (Bompiani, Milan 1958). 2. Wit and Wisdom of *Good Pope John*. Sayings and Stories. Collected by Henri Fesquet (orig. Les Fioretti du bon Pape Jean, Librairie Arthème Fayard, Paris 1964, with an Introduction by Christopher Butler, Abbot of Downside (Harwill Press, London, 1964). 3. *Libero Bigiaretti*, Le Indulgenze, (Bompiani, Rome, 1966). 4. *Ferruccio Ulivi*, La Livica del Carducci, Dai Primi Versi a 'Levia Gravia'. Saggio e Antologia, (Adriatica Editrice, Bari, 1968). 5. Also some covers for gramophone records such as for Ungaretti, Letture di Gian Carlo Sbragia, and others. 6. 35 Novelle Contemporanee. Selected and introduced by Delia Lennie, (Longmans, London, 1967. Cover to book). 7. La Carità Cristiana in Roma. A cura di Vincenzo Monachino (Cappelli, Bologna 1968. Cover and illustration). 8. Bianca Cordaro VI Parla di . . . Emilio Greco. (S.F. Flaccovio, Palermo, 1968. Cover.)

[1] Milan, 1965.

[2] Monsignore Giovanni Fallani used for his book *Dante Poeta Teologo* (Marzorati, Milan 1965) ten drawings by Emilio Greco from his illustrations to *La Divina Commedia*. The titles are: Paolo and Francesca, Francesca da Rimini, The Annunciation, Pia dei Tolomei, Ugo Capeto, Mathelda, The Good Shepherd, The Pilgrim, St John and Christ, The Virgin.

To complete the picture of his work, let us finally mention the smallest designs produced by the artist, the medals commissioned on various occasions. Their sizes range from $1\frac{1}{4}$ inches to $2\frac{1}{2}$ inches. There is the most beautiful memorial medal for the Prize Winners of the Quadrienale Exhibitions in Rome, showing the head and hands of a girl holding a flower (**52**). And there is the memorial medal produced for the opening of the Museum at Capodimonte in Naples, 1957. It represents a running nude holding a crystal, the symbol of perfection (**75**). Then followed, in 1959, the medal designed for the Olympiade in Rome 1960, again representing a running nude with a torch in her right hand, the five circles in the background, the symbol of the Olympiade. There is another model too with head, shoulders and arm of a girl, and the inscription: Parthenope (**74**).

There are two medals for the Autostrada del Sole, with the head of the sun god, Apollo, against a background of radiant sun rays.

The medal of the Comitato Romano, Messa Degli Artisti, with an angel's head and shoulders, his hand holding a chalice and a host; and further, the medal for the Mostra Antologica della Pittura e Scultura Italiana dal 1910 al 1930, with the finely incised head in profile of a girl and two hands, the right hand holding a branch of laurel.

There is the commemorative medal of the second Ecumenical Council of the Vatican of 1967, in gold, silver and bronze, representing an angel's head, bust and wings with the right hand raised in a gesture of oath; there is the medal and coin produced for the celebration of fifty years of Trieste's independence, 1968, in gold, silver and bronze, in two sizes representing in profile the head of Daphne – the symbol of liberty; and there is finally the commemorative medal of the centenary of Borromini produced in 1968.[1]

There are seventeen medals in all.

The artist also produced the plaque for the Rome Prize given to foreign artists. It is a relief $5\frac{1}{2}$ in. $\times$ 4 in., produced in 1963, and shows the head and shoulders of a girl in profile holding a pen. The muzzle of the Roman wolf faces the girl's head. For the Italian Nobel Prize (Premio Forte Dei Marmi) offered by the University of Pisa to foreigners who have distinguished themselves in cultural work concerning Italy, Greco produced a figure 1 ft $5\frac{3}{4}$ in. in height, representing a nude holding a palm leaf. This Prize is distributed yearly. It is made of gold and contains $1\frac{1}{2}$ kg of the precious metal. In 1965, the artist was commissioned by the Vatican to produce a model for a Vatican coin. It shows, on the obverse, the portrait of Pope Paul VI in profile with the Tiara (**70**), and, on the reverse side, the Good Shepherd carrying a sheep (**71**). A series of seven different pieces have been produced from this model. And speaking of commissions, let us not forget the four small and the two large angels produced for the Church of San Giovanni Bosco in Rome.

---

[1] 1 Giochi Della XVII Olimpiade Roma MCMLX. Diam: $2\frac{1}{8}$ in.

2 Autostrada Del Sole 1956-1964. Diam: $1\frac{1}{8}$ in. (An irregular circle.)

3 Museo e Gallerie Nazionali di Capodimonte. Napoli MCMLVII. Diam: $2\frac{1}{4}$ in.

4 Premio Nazionale di Paesaggio. Autostrada del Sole, Roma 1961.

5 VII Quadriennale Nazionale d'Arte. Mostra Antologica della Pittura e Scultura Italiane dal 1910 al 1930. Inscription in front: La Presidenza del Consiglio dei Ministri della Repubblica Italiana.

6 Lanificio Fratelli Cerruti. Biella 1881. Diam: $1\frac{1}{4}$ in.

7 Comitato Romano 'Messa degli Artisti MCMXLI. (Not signed.) Diam: $1\frac{1}{8}$ in.

8 VIII Quadriennale d'Arte. Maestri della Scuola Romana. Il Ministro della Pubblica Istruzione. Rome MCMLX. Diam: $1\frac{1}{4}$ in.

9 Parthenope. Inscription on reverse side of medal: Giochi Della XVII Olimpiade. Roma MCMLX.

10 Concilio Ecumenico Vaticano Secondo, 1962-1965. Inscription on reverse side of medal. Diam: 2 in. Silver One in gold for the Pope. Dedicated 'ad personam' to all the bishops of the Council.

11 Cinquantenario Della Redenzione, Trento e Trieste, 1918-1968. Inscription on reverse side of medal. Two sizes: diam: $1\frac{3}{4}$ in. and diam: $2\frac{1}{2}$ in. Gold, Silver and Bronze. Given to some authorities and soldiers of the First World War.

12 Borromini. Inscription on reverse side of medal. Outer circle: above, SPQR – XXI Aprill MCMLXVIII; below: MDCLXVII-MCMLXVII. Inner circle: Anno MMDCCXXI Di Roma – Centenario di Borromini. In the centre a shield with the letters SPQR in diagonal with a crown above it. Diam: 2 in. (An irregular circle.)

In 1960 Emilio Greco made a maquette for a monument in the Planck Institute at Munich in a competition in which three other artists took part. Although the Director of the Institute, Professor Werner Heisenberg was in favour of Greco's idea which expressed the flight of the human genius (a fountain with seagulls flying upwards) the design was not executed.

The artist has also designed ear-rings, bracelets, necklaces in precious metals, (studded with stones) as well as chandeliers and figures for door handles.

Emilio Greco has remained modest in spite of all his successes, childlike, often gay, though suffering from asthma, hay fever and arthritis, which he contracted in the damp studio of the Largo di Villa Massimo, the German Academy in Rome. He spent twelve years there. Then, when the Academy was returned to the German State in 1958, he was left without a studio. For some time he worked in the American Academy in Rome in the Via Angelo Masina (Porta S. Pancrazio).

Now, in his own studio which he has built for himself,[1] he has produced since May 1959 all the outstanding work which we have mentioned in the chapters of this book, always following the maxim that art is not scientific but poetical research. This is the creed by which he works and this is also the viewpoint which he applies when looking at the art of past ages or of our present time. He can take inspiration from anywhere. Japan and India had something to offer him, as had China for Marini: *All art epochs are good at their climax*, he once said. How different from the view of his time which prefers all primitive trends to anything else, Pop art, the a-formal, matter itself, the unfinished work, *l'art brut*. Among the moderns, Greco admires Picasso, above all as a graphic artist, Kokoschka, Martini, Marini and Manzù, the sculptures of Modigliani and Degas, to name only a few. As to his work, he can sigh: *The more I advance, the more I get disillusioned. I know my limits. When I was seventeen, I wished ardently to become a great artist. I still had illusions. Now, the more I become acknowledged, the stricter I am with myself. I like to teach, I like young people. I remember when, in 1945, I made portraits for the American soldiers for 1000 lire each, they were astonished to see someone working with his own hands. . . . I teach the young to see the human form, its harmony, not to look like a camera, mechanically.*[2]

Everything in nature can be seen and produced with a new vision. Something you can call style or invention. It comes from nature through our eyes into our soul and out again, filtered through human experience, through the personality of the artist, invented but true. I always demand from life a sensation. And even when the reality is no more, I demand a sensation of life from my memory. . . .

'Art', said Rodin 'is spiritualisation. It is the highest pleasure of the spirit which searches into nature and there divines the spirit by which nature herself is animated. It is the joy of the intellect which sees clearly into the Universe and which recreates it, with conscientious vision. Art is the most sublime mission of man, since it is the expression of thought seeking to understand the world and to make it understood'.[3]

Emilio Greco is an artist of whom Rodin could have approved. Preserving for his own time the true measure of greatness, his virtue is human dignity, his strength the high aspiration of man's spirit.

---

[1] In 1967 the artist built another studio at the seaside for reasons of health and absolute seclusion. (Lungomare Di Sabauda)
[2] Emilio Greco was Professor of Sculpture in Rome's *Liceo Artistico* 1948-1952, then in Carrara's *Accademia di Belle Arti* 1952-1955. In 1955, he was appointed for life to the Chair of Sculpture in Naple's *Accademia di Belle Arti*. He taught there until 1967. In 1959, he was also appointed Professor at the Munich Academy of Art, a Chair from which he had to resign in 1960 for reasons of health. The continual journeys from Rome to Munich were too exhausting. In 1961, he taught at Oskar Kokoschka's Summer Academy, *The School of Seeing*, in Salzburg. In 1966 he was appointed Professor of Sculpture at Rome Academy of Art.
[3] Auguste Rodin, Art. By Paul Gsell. op. cit.

Appendices

Biographical Notes

1913	Born in Catania, Sicily, the 11th October.
From 1927	Early work in Sicily as an apprentice and mate to a stone mason and sculptor of funerary monuments.
From 1933 onwards	Several visits to Rome.
1934-1935	Military Service in Palermo (18 months).
1934	Passes Examination at the Art Academy of Palermo (Licevo Artistico). Takes part in competitions and small exhibitions.
1939-1945	Military service during the war in Sicily, Albania and Rome.
1943	Leaves Sicily to settle in Rome.
1945	Marries Fernanda (Nanda) née De Andreis.
1948	Awarded the 'Premio S. Vincent'.
1948-1952	Appointed Professor of Sculpture at the Licevo Artistico in Rome.
1949	Daughter Antonella born the 14th October.
1952	Awarded the 'Premio del Parlamento' at the IV Quadriennale d'Arte in Rome.
1952-1955	Appointed Professor of Sculpture at the Accademia di Belle Arti in Carrara.
1953	Wins the Competition for the Monument to Pinocchio.
1955	Appointed Professor for life to the Chair of Sculpture in Naple's Accademia di Belle Arti. Taught there until 1967.
1956	Awarded the 'Premio del Comune di Venezia' on the occasion of the XXVIII Venice Biennale. Wins the Competition for the Monument to Engineer Camillo Olivetti. Creates Grande Bagnante I.
1959	Receives commission for the bronze doors of Orvieto Cathedral.
1959-1960	Appointed Professor of Sculpture at the Akademie der Bildenden Künste of Munich.
1960	Awarded the Great Gold Medal of Honour for the year 1960 on the occasion of the Spring Exhibition in the Künstlerhaus, Vienna. Awarded the Gold Medal 1st Class of the President of the Italian Republic 'Per i Benemeriti della Cultura e dell'Arte'.
1959-1964	Work on the Orvieto doors.
1961	Taught at Oskar Kokoschka's Summer Academy (School of Seeing) in Salzburg. Elected Honorary Member of the Akademie der Bildenden Künste, Munich.
1963	Nominated Corresponding Member of the Accademia di San Luca.
1965	Commissioned by Pope Paul VI to create the Monument to Pope John XXIII. Elected Accademico Nazionale by the President of the Italian Republic. Travels to his home town Catania in Sicily, also to Verona and Brescia. Journey to Hanover where he made a maquette for the museum and travelled on to Munich.
1965-1966	Work on the Monument to Pope John XXIII.
1966	With his daughter Antonella journied to Greece via Brindisi and Corfu to Igumenista, Patrasso, Olympia, Tripolis, Sparta, Mistras, Argos, Nauplion, Epidauros, Tolon, Daphne,

45

| 1967 | Athens, Sunion, Delphi, etc. (December). Journey to Sicily with his daughter to see again the old monuments particularly from the Greek period (6th Century BC). Appointed Professor of Sculpture at the Accademia di Belle Arti in Rome. | 1968 | Awarded the first prize offered by the Società Promotrice delle Belle Arti of Turin at the Quadriennale Nazionale there, (Exhibition 'Maestri Italiani'). Awarded La Tanagra d'Argento (small silver statue), Gran Premio della Promotrice Belle Arti per la Scultura. Journey to Sicily (Palermo, Segesta, Selinunte, Agrigento, Syracuse, Catania, Messina). |

1967 — Unveiling of the Monument to Pope John XXIII in St Peter's. Journey to Persia, (specifically visiting Teheran, and Isfahan).

1968 — Awarded the first prize of the VII Biennale dell' Incisione Italiana Contemporanea, Venice. Awarded the Premio della Calcografia offered by the Ministry of Public Instruction in Rome.

1968 — Awarded the first prize offered by the Società Promotrice delle Belle Arti of Turin at the Quadriennale Nazionale there, (Exhibition 'Maestri Italiani'). Awarded La Tanagra d'Argento (small silver statue), Gran Premio della Promotrice Belle Arti per la Scultura. Journey to Sicily (Palermo, Segesta, Selinunte, Agrigento, Syracuse, Catania, Messina).

1969 — Elected member of the Académié Royal de Belgique, Classe des Beaux-Arts. Second marriage, to Anna Padovan

1970 — Son Alessandro born 10 May

One Man and Retrospective Exhibitions[1]

Cities in Italy

Rome: Galleria Il Cortile (1946)
Galleria Il Secolo (1948)
VI Quadriennale di Roma (1952)
Galleria L'Obelisco (1954)
Galleria L'Obelisco (1957)
Ente Premi Roma, Palazzo Barberini, 1958.
Retrospective exhibition, 1938-1958.
Milan: Galleria Bergamini (1950)
Naples: Galleria S. Orsola (1950)
Florence: Galleria La Strozzina (Palazzo Strozzi, 1953)
Galleria Pananti (1969/70)
Venice: XXVIII Biennale (1956)
Pisa: Istituto di Storia dell'Arte dell' Università (1964)
Catania: Istituto di Storia dell'Arte dell' Università (1965)
Pescia: Palazzo di Valchiusa (Graphic works, 1968)
Ferrara: Galleria Civica d'Arte Moderna (1970)

[1] Emilio Greco has taken part in innumerable group exhibitions in almost all countries of Europe, North and South America as well as the Far East. (Exhibitions of large and small sculptures, drawings and graphic works. See Selected Bibliography, section Catalogues.)

International Cities

London: Roland, Browse & Delbanco (1952)
,, ,, ,, ,, (1955)
,, ,, ,, ,, (1959)

Antwerp: II Biennale of Sculpture (1953)
Rhode Island: Museum: (1954)
São Paulo: IV Biennale (1957)
Munich: Städtische Galerie (1959). Retrospective exhibition
Salzburg: Zwerglgarten (1959)
Vienna: Künstlerhaus (1960). Retrospective exhibition
Paris: Musée Rodin (1961). Retrospective exhibition
New York: The Contemporaries (1961)
Hiroshima: Fukuoka, and other cities in Japan (1961)
Tokyo: Shirokiya Foundation (1961) Retrospective exhibition
Takashimaya (1967)
Lisbon: Fundação Gulbenkian, (Gulbenkian Foundation, 1963). Retrospective exhibition.
Canberra: Albert Hall (1966)
Adelaide: National Gallery of South Australia (1966)
Melbourne: National Gallery of Victoria (1966)

Monuments and Other Works in Public Places

The Monument to Pinocchio	– in Collodi	The Bronze Doors for Orvieto	
The Monument to Engineer		Cathedral (Reliefs in Bronze)	– in Orvieto
Camillo Olivetti	– in Ivrea	The Olympian Victory	
Five Reliefs for the *Chiesa dell'*		The Monument to Pope John XXIII	
Autostrada del Sole, S. Giovanni		(Relief in Bronze) in	
Battista a Campi Bisenzio	– near Florence	St Peter's, Vatican	– in Rome
The Homecoming of Ulysses		Chiyoda Seimei Building	
(Relief) for the passenger		(Grande Bagnante)	– in Tokyo
ship *Michelangelo*.			

Works in Public Collections

Rome	Galleria Nazionale d'Arte Moderna	*Cologne*	Wallraf-Richartz-Museum
	Pinacoteca Vaticana	*Otterloo*	Rijksmuseum Kröller-Müller
Milan	Gabinetto Stampe	*St Louis*	City Art Museum
Venice	Galleria Internazionale d'Arte	*Cape Town*	South African National Gallery
	Moderna	*Toronto*	Art Gallery of Toronto
Milan	Galleria d'Arte Moderna	*Napier*	Art Gallery and Museum
Trieste	Museo Revoltella	*Adelaide*	National Gallery of South
Florence	Galleria d'Arte Moderna		Australia
Benevento	Museo del Sannio	*Melbourne*	National Gallery of Victoria
Lucca	Galleria Comunale	*Brisbane*	Queensland Art Gallery
Capri	Museo Michelangelo Caprese	*Worcester (USA)*	Art Museum
Paris	Musée National d'Art Moderne	*Los Angeles*	County Museum of Art
London	The Tate Gallery	*Auckland*	Art Gallery
Leicester	Museum and Art Gallery	*Tokyo*	Shirokiya Foundation
Birmingham	Museum	*Kyoto*	National Museum of Modern Art
Leeds	City Art Gallery	*Verona*	Galleria d'Arte Moderna
Brussels	Musée Royal des Beaux Arts	*Saarbrücken*	Saarland Museum
Antwerp	Musée Municipal de Sculpture en	*Bielefeld*	Kunsthalle der Stadt
	Plein Air	*Wuppertal*	Städtisches Museum
Duisburg	Museum	*Hagen*	Städtisches Ernst-Osthaus Museum
Munich	Neue Pinakothek	*Mannheim*	Kunsthalle
	Staatliche Münzsammlung	*Karlsruhe*	Badisches Landesmuseum

Select Bibliography

1 Books

Giuseppe Selvaggi   *Scoperta dell' Europa*. Danesi, Rome, September, 1948.

Fortunato Bellonzi   *Emilio Greco*. Instituto Grafico Tiberino, Rome, 1949.

James Thrall Soby and Alfred H Barr (jr.)   *Twentieth-Century Italian Art*. The Museum of Modern Art, New York, 1949.

Roberto Salvini   *Guida All' Arte Moderna*. Garzanti, Milan, 1951.

Emilio Greco   *Poesie*. Fiumara, Milan, 1952.

Leonardo Sciascia   *Il Pinocchio di E. Greco*. Caltanissetta, 1954.

Luigi Volpicelli   *La Veritá su Pinocchio e Saggio sul' cuore*. Armando, Rome, 1954.

Henry Schaefer-Simmern   *Sculpture in Europe Today*. University of California Press, Berkeley & Los Angeles, 1955.

Eduard Trier   *Zeichner des Zwanzigsten Jahrhunderts*. Büchergilde Gutenberg, Frankfurt am Main; and Verlag Gebr. Mann, Berlin, 1956.

Bernhard Degenhart   *Italienische Zeichner der Gegenwart*. Verlag Gebr. Mann, Berlin, 1956.

Dizionario Enciclopedico Italiano   *Text on Greco* by Marco Valsecchi. Instituto della Enciclopedia Italiana, Rome, 1956.

Emilio Lavagnino   *L'Arte Moderna Dai Neoclassici ai Contemporanei*, 2 vols. Unio Tipografico – Editrice Torinese, Turin, 1956.

Giovanni Carandente   *Scultura Italiana del XX Secolo*. Editalia, Rome, 1957.

Teiichi Hijikata   *Scultura Italiana Contemporanea*. Zauho Kankokai, Tokyo, 1957.

Vincenzo Ciardo   *Quasi un Diario*. Mele, Naples, 1957.

Mario De Micheli   *Scultura Italiana del Dopoguerra*. Schwarz, Milan, 1958.

Leopold Zahn   *Eine Geschichte der Modernen Kunst, Malerei, Plastik, Architektur*. Ullstein, Berlin, 1958.

Wolfgang Braunfels   *Meisterwerke Europäischer Plastik von der Antike bis zur Gegenwart*. Atlantis, Zurich, 1958.

Werner Hofmann   *Die Plastik des 20 Jahrhunderts*. Fischer Bücherei, Frankfurt am Main, Hamburg, 1958.

Neue Kunst nach 1945. Edited by Will Grohmann.   'Italien'. Text by Giulio Carlo Argan and Nello Ponente. Verlag M. DuMont Schauberg, Cologne, 1958.

Olivetti 1908–1958.   Ing. C. Olivetti P.C. S.p.A., Ivrea, 1958.

Fortunato Bellonzi   *L'Arte nel Secolo della Tecnica*. De Luca, Rome, 1958.

Fortunato Bellonzi – Valerio Mariani   *Il Pinocchio Di Emilio Greco*. De Luca, Rome, 1958.

Art Since 1945.   'Italy'. Text by Giulio Carlo Argan and Nello Ponente. Thames and Hudson London, 1958.

Daniele Grassi   *Emilio Greco, Plastiken und Zeichnungen*. Piper Bücherei, R. Piper Verlag, Munich, 1959.

John Cairncross   *By a Lonely Sea, Translations and Poems*. Hong Kong University Press, 1959.

Tetsuo Abe   *Moulders of Modern Form, Looking at Europe's Forefront of Art*. The Mainichi Newspaper Publishing Co., Tokyo, 1959.

Guido Perocco   *La Galleria d'Arte Moderna di Venezia*. Istituto Italiano d'Arti Grafiche, Bergamo, 1959.

Emile Langui — *50 Jahre Moderne Kunst.* Verlag M. DuMont Schauberg, Cologne, 1959.

Michel Seuphor — *La Sculpture de ce Siècle.* Editions du Griffon, Neuchâtel, 1959.

L'Arte Dopo il 1945. — *Italia, Giulio Carlo Argan e Nello Ponente.* Ed. Il Saggiatore, Milan, 1959.

Dictionnaire de la Sculpture Moderne. Edited by Roland Maillard. — Fernand Hazan, Paris, 1960.

Garibaldo Marussi — *Disegno Italiano Moderno.* Sandro Maria Rosso, Biella, 1960.

Ennio Francia — *Pinacoteca Vaticana.* Aldo Martello, Milan, 1960.

Eduard Trier — *Figur und Raum, Die Skulptur des XX Jahrhunderts.* Gebr. Mann Verlag, Berlin, 1960.

Personaggi delle Arti Figurative A–Z Index — Zanichelli, Bologna, 1960.

Bernhard Degenhart — *Emilio Greco.* Florian Kupferberg Verlag, Mainz-Berlin, 1960.

Renato Civello — *Occasioni Figurative.* Maia, Siena, 1960.

Enciclopedia Italiana, Appendix III, A–L, 1949–1960. — Istituto della Enciclopedia Italiana, Rome, 1961.

Eduard Trier — *Figura e Spazio, La Scultura del XX Secolo.* Capelli, Bologna, 1961.

Ennio Francia — *Modern Paintings and Sculptures in the Vatican Collections.* Lorenzo del Turco, Rome, 1961.

Roberto Salvini — *Scultura Italiana Moderna* Silvana, Milan, 1961.

Tito Miotti — *Il Collezionista di Disegni,* Neri Pozza, Venice, 1962.

Werner Hofmann — *La Scultura del XX Secolo.* Capelli, Rome, 1962.

A Dictionary of Modern Sculpture. Editor Robert Maillard. — Text on Greco by Giovanni Carandente. Methuen, London 1962.

Grandi Disegni di Ogni Tempo, Vol. I. Italiani — Text on Greco by Winslow Ames. Valentino Bompiani, Milan, 1962.

Enciclopedia Garzanti, Vol. I — Garzanti, Milan, 1963.

Bino Sanminiatelli — *Il Permesso di Vivere (A Diary).* Valentino Bompiani, Milan, 1963.

Carlo Ceschi — *La Chiese di Roma Dagli Inizi del Neoclassico al 1961.* Capelli, Rome, 1963.

Virgilio Cuzzi — *Arte D'Oggi – Storia di 8 Biennali.* Canesi, Rome, 1964.

Herbert Read — *A Concise History of Modern Sculpture.* Thames & Hudson, London, 1964.

Enzo Carli, Gian Alberto Dell'Acqua — *Profilo dell' Arte Italiana, I/III* Istituto Italiano d'Arti Grafiche, Bergamo, 1964.

Guido Ballo — *La Linea Dell' Arte Italiana.* Méditerranèe, Rome, 1964.

La Chiesa dell' Autostrada del Sole — *S. Giovanni Battisto A Campi Bisenzio.* Firema, Rome, 1964.

Father Ethrington — *The Church and Art.* Hows, Printers, London, 1964.

Guiseppe Maimone — *Elementi di Anatomia Artistica, Part III.* Edizione della Rassegna, Naples, 1965.

Carlo Munari — *100 Disegni di 25 Artisti Italiani.* Documenti Contemporanei. Sipra, Turin, 1965.

'J P Hodin – European Critic'. — *Essays by Various Hands.* Edited by Walter Kern. Cory, Adams and Mackay, 1965.

Ennio Francia — *La Via Crucis nella Interpretazione di un gruppo di Scultori Romani,* Aldo Martello, Milan, 1965.

Palma Bucarelli — *Sculturi Italiani Contemporanei.* Martello, Milan, 1967.

Giovanni Fallani — *Papa Giovanni di Emilio Greco.* Editalia, Rome, 1967.

I Maestri del Disegno Contemporanei, 1940–1965. — Edited by E. Johnson. Bompiani, Milan, 1967 (New York 1964).

L'attività della Santa Sede Nel 1967. — Tipografia Poliglotta, Vatican, Rome, 1967.

Cesare Bobba — *Monete Papalia da Pio VII a Paolo VI.* Stato Pontificio e Città del Vaticano. Asti, 1967.

Carlo Pirovano — *Scultura Italiana Dal Neoclassicismo Alle Correnti Contemporanee.* Electa, Milan, 1968.

Bianca Cordaro (VI) — *. . . Parla di Emilio Greco.* S. F. Flaccovio, Palermo, 1968.

Museo Internazionale d'Arte Contemporanea. — Florence, Palazzo Vecchio. Marchi e Bertolli, Florence, 1967.

Jean Cassou — *Beispiele Moderner Plastiken . . . etc.* Art – C. C. Verlag, Galerie Christoph Czwiklitzer. (No date.)

2 Periodicals

Leonida Rèpaci — La Scultura alla IV Quadriennale. *L'Illustrazione Italiana, Milan,* 13 June 1943.

Mario Negri — Sculture di Greco. *Domus* No. 254, Milan, January 1951.

Jacopo Recupero — Emilio Greco. *Tour Italy,* No. 7-8, New York, July–August, 1951.

Giuseppe Marchiori — Discorso sulla Quadriennale. *La Fiera Letteraria,* Rome, 16th December 1951.

Ferruccio Ulivi — Pagina per Emilio Greco. *Galleria,* Salvatore Sciascia, Caltanissetta, January, 1953.

Valerio Mariani — Scultura di Greco. *Idea,* Rome, 2nd June 1954.

J P Hodin — Emilio Greco. *Kroniek van Kunst en Kultuur,* Amsterdam, No. 3. March, 1954.

J P Hodin — Emilio Greco. *The Studio,* London, April 1954.

J P Hodin — Portrait of the Artist, Emilio Greco. *Art News and Review.* London, No. 6. April 1954.

P Pik (J P Hodin) — An Italian Sculptor at Work. *Art,* Vol. I, No. 23, London, September 1955.

Carlo Ludovico Ragghianti — Emilio Greco. *Sele-Arte,* No. 24, Florence, May-June 1956.

Virgilio Guzzi — Pinocchio Preserved. *Life,* New York, Vol. 40, No. 23, June 1956.

Mario Monteverdi — Gli Equivoci della XXVIII Biennale. *Arte Figurativa,* No. 4, Milan, July–August 1956.

Lisa Licitra Ponti — Impressioni di un Visitatore alla Biennale. *Domus,* Milan, September 1956.

Rodolfo Pallucchini — La XXVIII Biennale de Venise. *Prisme des Arts,* No. 5, Paris, October 1956.

Guido Perocco — I Moderni Italiani A Londra. *La Fiera Letteraria,* Rome, 30th December, 1956.

J P Hodin — Emilio Greco. *Das Kunstwerk,* No. 1-2, Baden-Baden, 1956/57.

L Ronchi — Monumento a Pinocchio a Collodi. *L'Architettura,* No. 17, Rome, March, 1957.

Inaugurato a Ivrea il monumento all'ing. Olivetti. — Notizie Olivetti, October 1957.

Eduard Trier — Pinoquio e o seu Autor têm um Monumento Pago Pelas Criancas de Todo o Mundo Seculo, 3rd February, 1957.

Giorgio Kaisserlian — In Bronze and Marble. *Time,* New York, 12th May, 1958.

M Pardo — Note su Una Mostra de Emilio Greco, Galleria Sciascia, Caltanissetta - Rome, May/June, 1958.

Lionello Venturi — Arte Moderna a Bruxelles. *L'Espresso,* Rome, 8th June, 1958.

J P Hodin — Emilio Greco. *Kunst og Kultur,* No. 2, Oslo, 1958.

Eric Newton — Emilio Greco. *Time and Tide,* London, 26th September, 1959.

Giovanni Fallani — Omaggio a Dante. *Ecclesia,* Vatican City, February 1960.

Alfredo Entita — Lo Scultore Emilio Greco. *Tecnica e Ricostruzione,* No. 5-6, Catania, May-June 1960.

Deoclecio Redig De Campos — Arte Contemporanea nella Pinacoteca Vaticana. *Ecclesia,* Vatican City, October 1960.

Mario Quattro Ciocchi — Arte Italiana nel Mondo. *Nuova Antologia,* Rome, part 4, 1927, July 1961.

A Heldt — Emilio Greco. Das Schönste, *Kindler und Schiermeyer,* No. 12, Munich, December 1961.

Y Yanagihara — Sculpture of Emilio Greco. *The Sansai Fine Art Magazine,* Tokyo, 1962.

F Miwa — Lessons of Emilio Greco. *Mizue,* Bijiutsu Shuppan-Sha, Tokyo, n.682, January 1962.

Guido Burganda — Emilio Greco. *Estudos Italianos em Portugal,* No. 21/22, 1962/63.

Carlo Ludovico Ragghianti — Artisti Italiani. *Sele-Arte,* Ed. Olivetti, Florence, May-June 1963.

Gustav René Hocke — Die Herz-Dome Italiens und die Moderne Kunst. *Die Tat,* Zurich, 6th March, 1964.

Fortunato Bellonzi — Le Porte del Duomo di Orvieto. *La Nuova Antologia,* Rome, January 1964.

Fortunato Bellonzi — Sono Nate a Roma Le Porte Per Orvieto. *Capitolium,* Rome, February 1964.

Fortunato Bellonzi — Polemica per le Porte del Duomo di Orvieto. *Le Arti*, Milan, April 1964.

Sigfrido Maovaz — Le Porte di Greco per il Duomo di Orvieto. *Civiltà dello Spirito*, Rome, June, 1964.

Mario Pepe — Sulle Porte per il Duomo di Orvieto, *Rassegna di Cultura e Vita Scolastica*, Rome, 1st March, 1964.

Giuliana Zavadini — Le Porte del Duomo di Orvieto: Intervista con Emilio Greco. *Civiltà delle Macchine*, Rome, January-February 1964.

J P Hodin — Greco's Doors at Orvieto. *Apollo*, London, March 1964.

B H V Graefe — Neue Pforten Öffnen Sich. *Europa*, No. 176, Nürnberg, August 1964.

Carlo Ludovico Ragghianti — Storie di Porte di Cattedrali. *Critica d'Arte*, Florence, vol. 61, 1964.

J P Hodin — Emilio Greco – Doomtüren für Orvieto. *Die Kunst und das Schöne Heim*, Munich, No. 8, May 1965.

J P Hodin — Emilio Greco – The Earthly and the Heavenly Love, *Studio International*, London, No. 869, September, 1965.

R M De Angelis — Panorama della IX Quadriennale. *Notiziaro d'Arte*, Rome, Jan/Feb 1966.

Japan Interior Design — Tokyo No. 41. August 1966. (illus).

The Japan Architect — Tokyo, August 1966 (illus).

The Kindai Kenechiku — *Magazine of Contemporary Architecture*, volume 20, No. 8. Tokyo, August 1966.

Mariarosa Carreri — La Riscoperta dell' Inspirazione Femminile. *Domina*, Year I, No. 6, Rome, August 1966.

Il Concilio Vaticano II — No. 3, November 1966. Fratelli Fabbri, Milan.

Giovanni Fallani — Il Papa Giovanni di Emilio Greco. *Civiltà delle Macchine*, No. 5, Rome, Sept/Oct 1966.

Ivana Montana Mononi — *La Inserción de Obras Contemporáneas En un Contexto Antiguo. Goya, Revistade Arte*, No. 77, Madrid, 1967.

3 Catalogues

Nicola Ciarletta — *Emilio Greco.* 'Cortile', Rome, 1946.

Carlo Barbieri — *Emilio Greco.* Galleria 'S. Orsola', Naples, 1950.

First Exhibition in England — *Emilio Greco.* Roland, Browse and Delbanco, April-May 1952.

F Bandonin — *II Biennale de la Sculptura.* II Biennale, Middelheim Park, Antwerp, 1953.

Carlo Ludovico Ragghianti — *Emilio Greco.* 'La Strozzina', Florence, 1953.

Palma Bucarelli — *Arte Italiana Contemporanea.* Bienal Hispano-Americana de Arte, Madrid, May-June 1955.

John Maxon — *Drawings by Emilio Greco.* Museum of Art, Rhode Island School of Design, 15th November–15th December 1954.

L'Obelisco 1955. — Galleria l'Obelisco, Rome, 1955.

Recent Sculpture by Emilio Greco — Roland, Browse and Delbanco, September-October 1955.

Giorgio Castelfranco — *Emilio Greco.* XXVIII Venice Biennale, 1956.

Umbro Apollonio — *Artistas Italianos De Hoje.* IV Bienal do Museo de Arte Moderna de São Paulo, Brazil, September-December 1957.

Franco Russoli — *Mit Italienischen Bildhauern.* Neue Darmstädter Sezession, Darmstadt, October-November 1957.

Carlo Munari — *Greco.* Centro Culturale Canavesano, Ivrea, 1958.

Enzo Carli — *Emilio Greco.* Ente Premi Roma, Rome, 1958.

50 Ans d'Art Moderne — *Exposition Universelle et Internationale de Bruxelles*, Palais International des Beaux Arts, 1958.

Bernhard Degenhart — *Emilio Greco.* Städtische Galerie München, Munich, 16th January–15th February, 1959.

Berhard Degenhart   *Emilio Greco*. Würtembergischer Kunstverein, Stuttgart, 16th April–7th May, 1959.

J P Hodin   *Emilio Greco*. Bronzes and Drawings. Roland, Browse and Delbanco, London, September–October 1959.

Gian Alberto Dell' Acqua   *Peintres et Sculpteurs Italiens du Futurisme à nos Jours.* Exhibition of Italian Art organised by the Venice Biennale, 1959.

Ronald Alley   *The Foreign Paintings, Drawings and Sculpture.* The Tate Gallery, London, 1959.

Catalogue Middelheim   1959.

Rodolfo Pallucchini   *Sculpture Italienne Contemporaine d' Arturo Martini À Nos Jours.* Musée Rodin, Paris, 1960.

The Tate Gallery Report   London, 1960–61.

J P Hodin   *Emilio Greco. Sculptures and Drawings.* The Contemporaries, New York, March, 1961.

Maurilio Coppini   *Sculpture of Emilio Greco.* Foundation Shirokiya, Tokyo, 1961.

SPQR   Galleria Communale d'Arte Moderna. Prima Mostra di una selezione di Opere. Palazzo delle Esposizioni, Rome, 1963.

Guido Burgada   *Emilio Greco.* Gulbenkian Foundation, Lisbon, 1963.

Ida Cardellini   *Emilio Greco: Opera Grafica.* Istituto di Storia dell'Arte dell'Università di Pisa. Pisa, 15th June–15th July, 1964.

Ottavio Morisani   *Mostra di Emilio Greco.* Istituto di Storia dell'Arte della Università di Catania. Catania, February–March 1965.

Arbeiten des Bildhauers Emilio Greco.   Akademie der bildenden Künste, Munich, May, 1965.

XXIV Biennale Nazionale d'Arte.   Città Di Milano, Palazzo della Permanente, Milan, May–October, 1965.

Catalogo Bolaffi   Il Collezionista d'Arte Moderna. Giulio Bolaffi, Turin, 1966.

Catalogo Nazionale dei Francobolli Italiani, 1966.   Edizioni Scot, Bolaffi, Turin, 1966.

Fortunato Bellonzi   Arte Italiano Contemporáneo desde 1900. Museo de Arte Moderno, Mexico, 1966.

Arte Italiano Contemporáneo   Centro America 1967. Exposición Itinerante organised by the 'Quadriennale d'Arte' in Rome. July–December 1967.

C L Ragghianti   *XVIII Mostra Internazionale d' Arte, Premio del Fiorino.* Palazzo Strozzi, Florence, 1967.

Mario de Biasi   *VI Biennale dell' Incisione Italiana Contemporanea.* Opera Bevilacqua La Masa, Venice, 1968.

Galleria Communale d'Arte Moderna, Civitanova Alta, 1968.   (Memorial Exhibition for for Marco Moretti.)

Mostra del Disegno Contemporaneo.   *Disegni di Scultori Italiani.* Bassano del Grappe, 1968.

VIII Biennale Nazionale d'Arte Sacra Contemporanea.   *Premio Federico Motta.* Rome, Bologna, 1968. Milan, Genova, 1969. Federico Motta Editore.

Come visitare il Vaticano. How to Visit the Vatican.   Rome. (No date.)

C L Ragghianti   *Emilo Greco. Donazione al Museo Internazionale d'Arte Moderna di Firenze e alla Pinacoteca Vaticana.* Galleria Pananti, Florence, 20 December 1969 – 13 January 1970.

4 Calendars

Atsuo Imaizumi   The Sculpture of Emilio Greco, A Calendar. Mizue, Tokyo, 1956.
Sculpture of Emilio Greco, A Calendar. Tokyo, 1962.
Bijutsu Shuppah-sha (The Fine Arts Publishing Co.) Tokyo. Calendar 1966.

5 Films

In 1966 five films were made on the sculptures of Emilio Greco of which two were documentary on the work in progress of the monument to Pope John XXIII (Producer Mr Alliata). They were shown on TV programmes in Italy, England, France and Germany.

Catalogue of Illustrations

I ILLUSTRATIONS IN THE TEXT

II COLOUR PLATES

III MONOCHROME ILLUSTRATIONS

Sculpture

146 Annabelle, 1965. Indian Ink, 24 × 28 in. *Collection the artist*

147 Claudia, 1963. Indian Ink, 15½ × 20 in. *Collection Silvano Giannelli, Rome*

148 Dog, 1961. Indian Ink, 28 × 20 in. *Collection Leonardo Sciascia, Palermo*

149 Study of Large Bather I, 1956. Indian Ink, 26½ × 19 in. *Tate Gallery, London*

150 Study of Pinocchio, 1953. Indian Ink, 26½ × 19 in. *Tate Gallery, London*

151 Study of Pinocchio, 1953. Indian Ink, 26½ × 19 in. *Tate Gallery, London*

152 Sketch for the Monument, 'The Elevation of the Soul of Man', 1956. Indian Ink, 26½ × 19 in. *Collection the artist*

153 Wrestler, 1948. Indian Ink, 20 × 14 in. *Galleria Nazionale d'Arte Moderna, Rome*

154 Portrait of Pope John XXIII, 1962. Study for Centre Door of Orvieto Cathedral. Indian Ink, 28 × 20 in. *Pinacoteca Vaticana, Rome*

155 St John and Christ, 1959. Illustration for Dante's 'Divine Comedy', Paradiso, Canto XXVI. Indian Ink, 20 × 14 in. *Pinacoteca di Ravenna*

156 Thaïs, 1958. Illustration for Dante's 'Divine Comedy', Inferno, Canto XVIII. Indian Ink, 26½ × 19 in. *Pinacoteca di Ravenna*

157 Bust of a Young Woman, 1961. Indian Ink, 21 × 14 in. *Collection the artist*

158 Woman Combing her Hair, 1961. Indian Ink, 28 × 20 in. *Collection the artist*

159 Erica, 1961. Indian Ink, 28 × 20 in. *Collection the artist*

160 Illustration for Ovid's *Ars Amatoria*, 1968. Indian Ink. *Museo Internazionale d'Arte Contemporanea, Florence*

161 Illustration for Ovid's *Ars Amatoria*, 1968. Indian Ink. *Museo Internazionale d'Arte Contemporanea, Florence*

1 The Artist in his studio in Rome, 1965

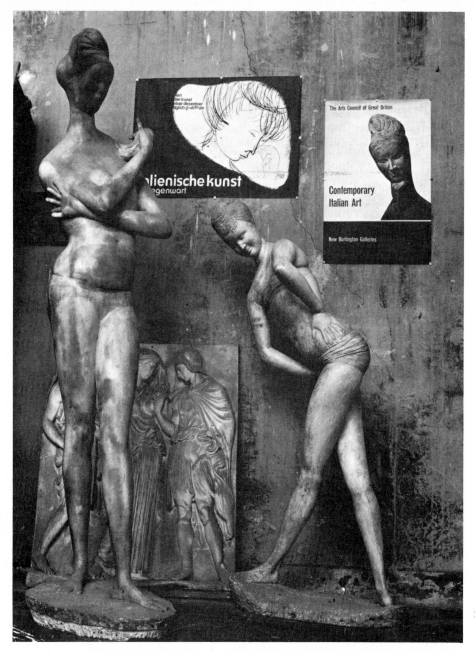

2 A corner of the Artist's old studio, Villa Massimo,
with originals of Large Bather I (foreground)
and Large Bather III

3 Retrospective Exhibition, Palazzo Barberini, Rome 1958.
Centre, Large Bather (left to right) III, I and II

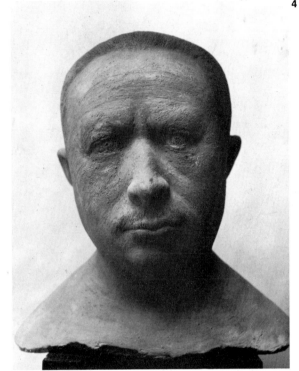

4

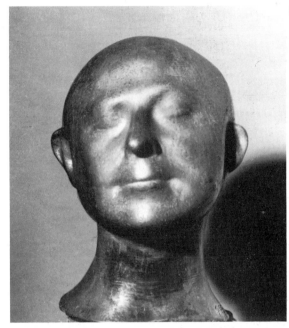

5

6

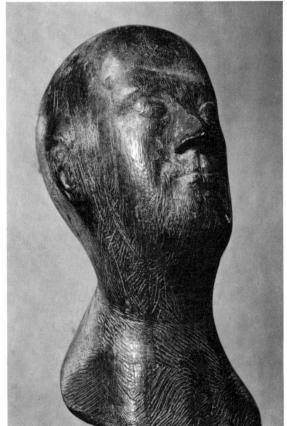

7

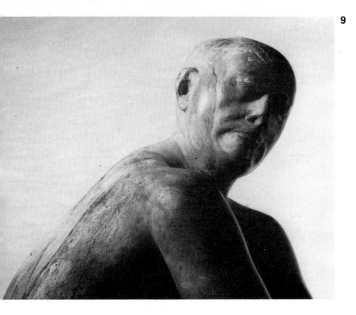

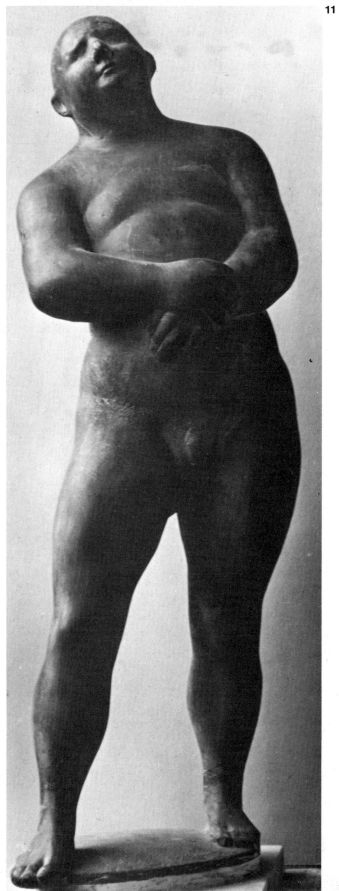

8 **Large Wrestler,** *(detail)* **1947/48**

9 **Sitting Man** *(detail),* **1962**

10 **Wrestler, 1947**

11 **The Singer, 1947**

12   The Ox, 1948

13 Dying Horse, 1949

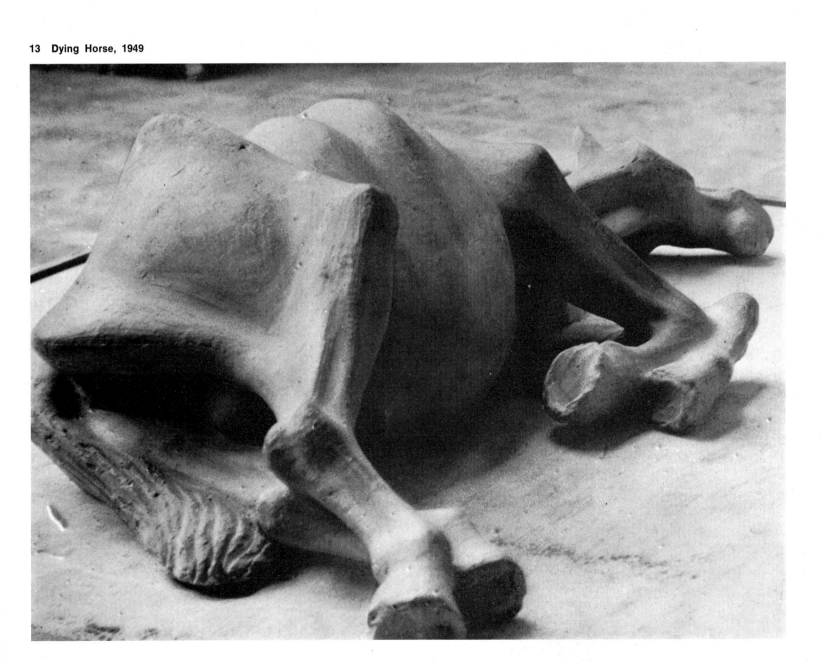

14 Pamela I, 1954

15 Portrait, 1952

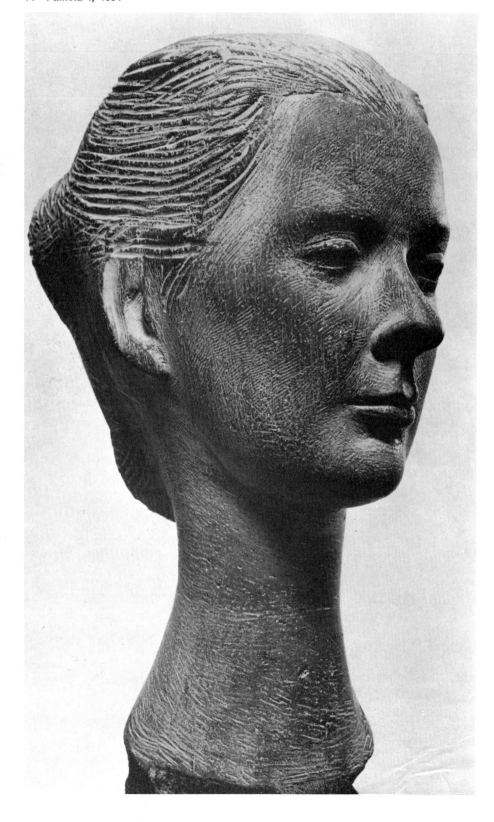

16 Seated Figure, 1949

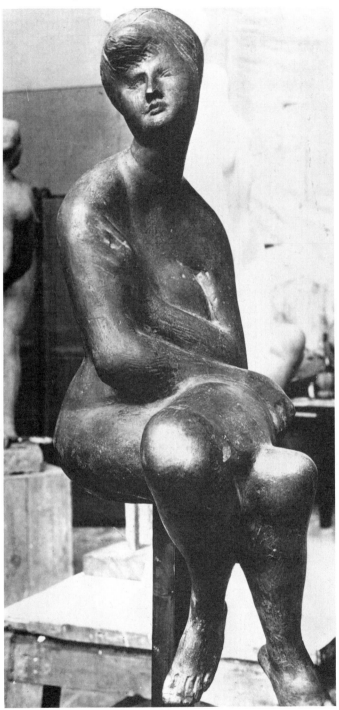

17 Fiorella, 1949

18 Zenobia, 1954

19   Malgari Onnis, 1953

20   Woman of Trieste, 1954

21 Head of the Fairy (Pinocchio), 1953

23   Head of a Woman, 1957

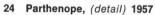

24   Parthenope, *(detail)* **1957**

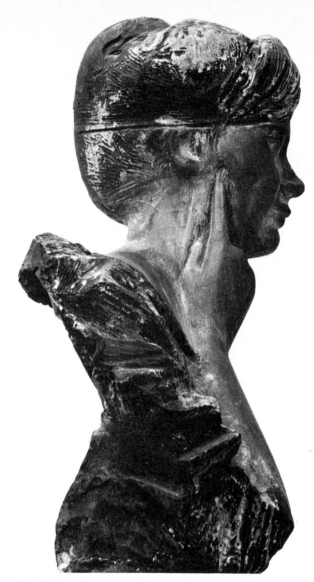

25   Marisa Ciardiello, 1958

I   Head of a Man, 1965

II   Head of a Woman, 1951

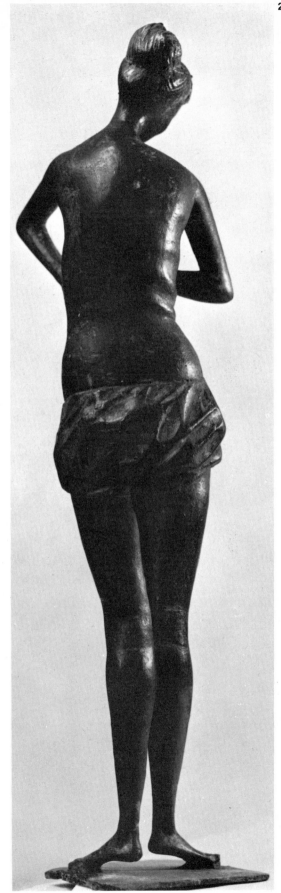

26 Chiara, *(detail)* 1959

27 Group of Dancers, 1955

28 Dancer I, 1955

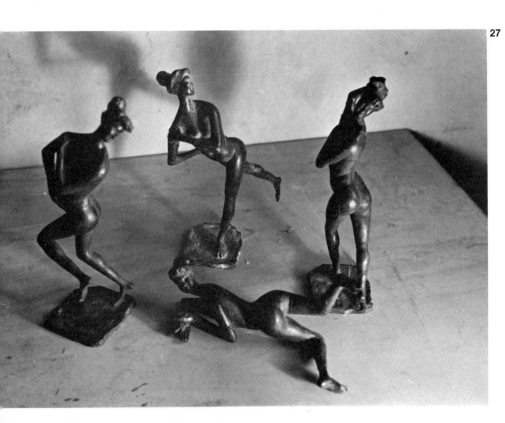

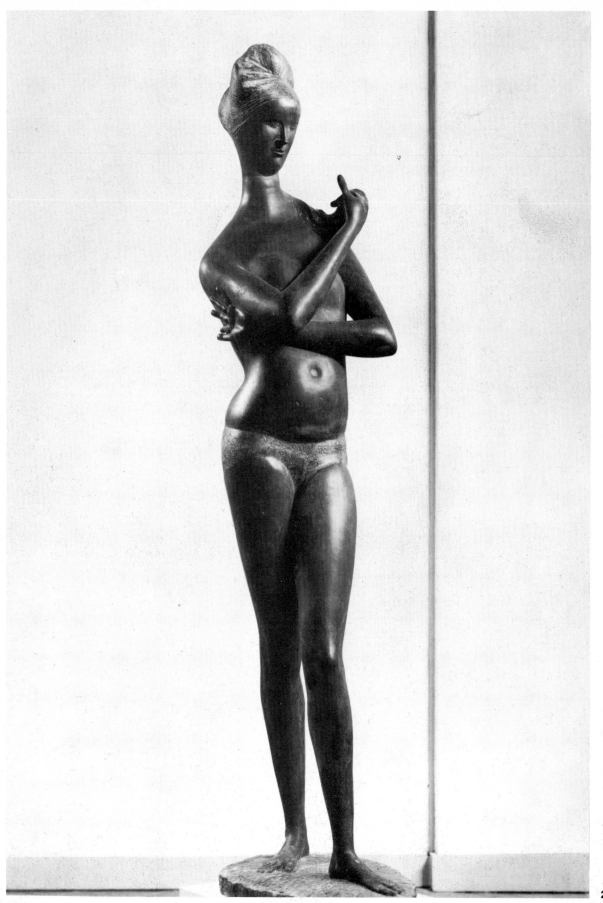

29 Large Bather I, 1956

31 Large Bather I, *(detail)*

30 Large Bather I, *(side-view)*

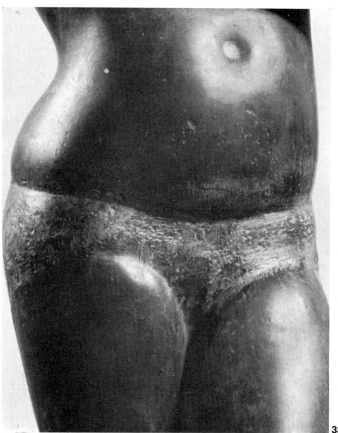

33

32 **Large Bather I,** *(detail)*

33 **Large Bather I,** *(detail)*

34 **Large Bather II, 1956/57**

36   Large Bather III, *(front-view)* **1957**

37   Large Bather III, *(side-view)*

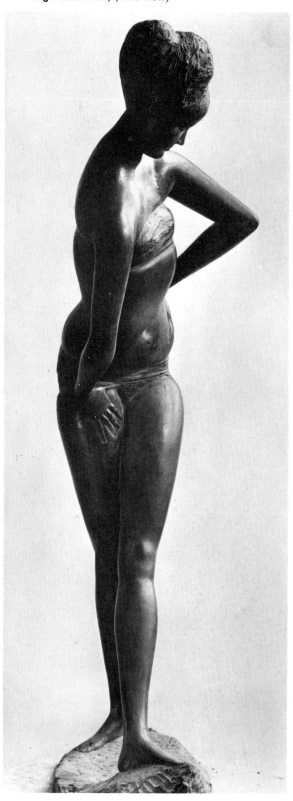

39   **Large Bather IV,** *(back-view)* **1959**
40   **Large Bather IV,** *(front-view)*
41   **Large Bather IV,** *(detail)*

41

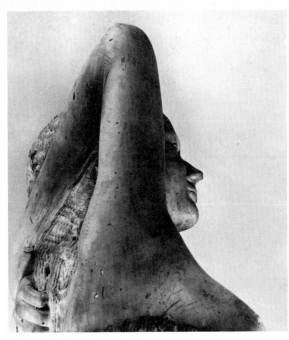

42 **Portrait of Anna,** *(detail)*

43 **Portrait of Anna 1962**

III **Portrait of Anna, 1962** *(detail)*

IV The Artist with Large Seated Figure of 1951 in his garden in Rome

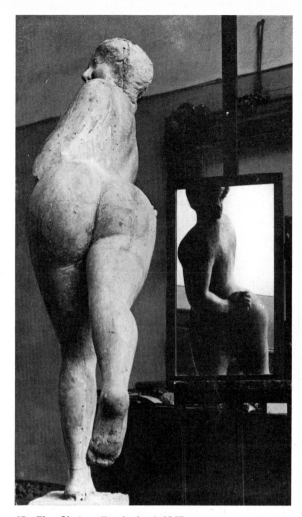

45   The Skater, *(back-view)* 1947

44   The Cyclist, 1947

47 Figure, 1950

48   **Olympian Victory, 1960**

49   **Olympian Victory, in situ by night**

50   **Olympian Victory,** *(detail)*

V Olympian Victory, 1960 *(detail)*

VI Large Bather VI, 1962/64 *(detail)*

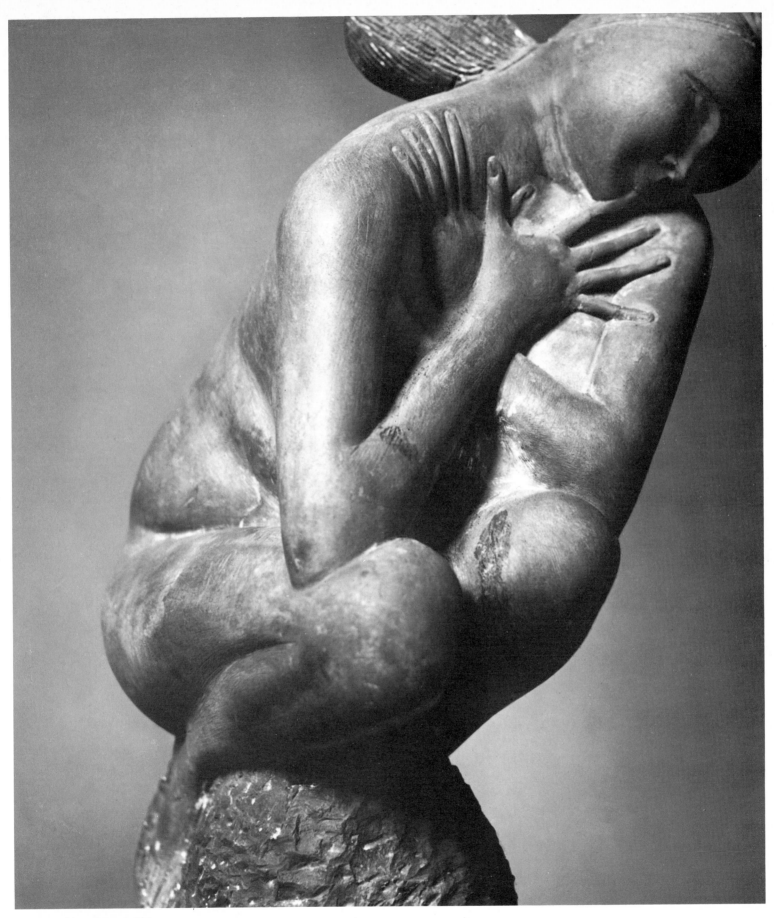

51 Crouching Figure, 1956

52 Study of Hands, 1960 *(detail from Quadrinale Medal)*

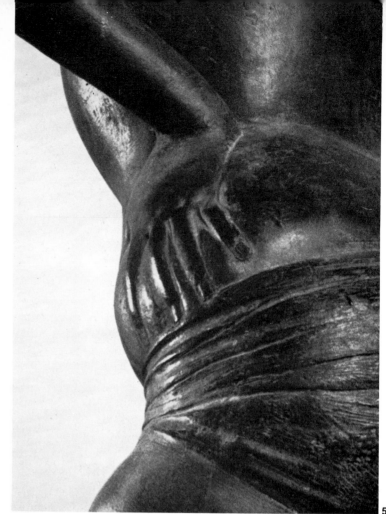

53

54

53 Study of Hands, 1957 *(detail from Large Bather III)*

54 Study of Hands, 1956 *(detail from Large Bather I)*

55 Study of Hands, 1960 *(detail from Olympian Victory)*

56 Study of Hands, 1956 *(detail from Marisa)*

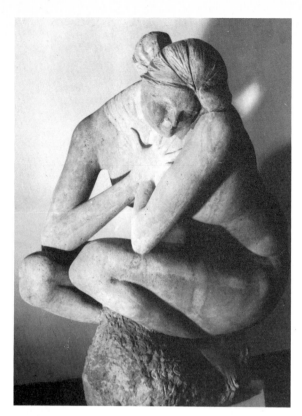

57 **Large Crouching Figure,** 1961

58 **Large Crouching Figure,** *(detail)*

59 **Crouching Figure I,** 1953

60 Aretusa, 1954

61 Pamela II, 1964

62 *(opposite)* **Large Nude, 1952**

63 **Large Nude, 1952** *(detail)*

64 **Anna, 1954**

65 Iphigenia, 1961

66 Luna, 1961

VII Onoria, 1965

VIII   Eiko, 1968

67 Face of Bather, 1961

68 Marta, 1965

69 Monument to Camillo Olivetti, 1957

70 Portrait of Pope Paul VI, 1965

71 The Good Shepherd, 1965
    (reverse side of Vatican Coin)

72 Medal for Seventh Quadrienale
    Nazionale d'Arte, Rome, 1955

73 Model for medal in
    commemoration of
    17th Olympiad, Rome, 1960

70

72

71

73

74   Medal with Parthenope,
     17th Olympiad, Rome, 1960

75   Medal for the Museum of
     Capodimonte, Naples, 1957

76 Monument to Pinocchio, 1953/56

77 Monument to Pinocchio, *(back-view)*

78 Monument to Pinocchio, *(detail)*

79 Monument to Pinocchio, *(detail)*

80 Monument to Pinocchio, *(base)*

81 S. Ambrogio Besieged
in the Basilica Porzia,
1960/61

82 S. Ambrogio, *(detail)*

IX   The Five Reliefs in the Church of S. Giovanni Battista
       a Campi Bisenzio, Florence, 1960/61

**X   The Episode of S. Ambrogio Teaching the Singing of His
Hymms to the Faithful Imprisoned with Him, 1960/61,** *(detail)*

83 S. Geminiano: Exorcism
    of the Daughter of the Emperor
    Gioviano, 1960/61

84 S. Geminiano, *(detail)*

85 S. Chrisanto & S. Daria:
Martyrdom of the Wedded Pair, 1960/61

86 The Mass of S. Ilario of Poitiers, 1960/61

87 The Mass of S. Ilario, *(detail)*

88 Martyrdom of S. Giustina, 1960/61

89 Martyrdom of S. Giustina, *(detail)*

90   The Samaritan, *(detail)* 1950

91   Return of Ulysses, 1964

92 Orvieto Cathedral. The huge doors
by Emilio Greco were produced in 1961/64

93 Centre Door of Orvieto Cathedral, *(detail)*

94 Centre Door of Orvieto Cathedral,
Episode, To Clothe the Naked

95 Centre Door of Orvieto Cathedral,
Episode, To Comfort the Imprisoned

96 Centre Door of Orvieto Cathedral,
Episode, To Bury the Dead.

98 Centre Door of Orvieto Cathedral,
Episode, To Feed the Hungry and Give Drink to the Thirsty

97 Centre Door of Orvieto Cathedral,
Episode, To Feed the Hungry and
Give Drink to the Thirsty

99 Centre Door of Orvieto Cathedral,
Episode, To Harbour the Homeless

XI To Visit the Sick, 1961/64

XII   Design and Stamps for Vatican postage, 1963

**100 Centre Door of Orvieto Cathedral,
Episode, To Harbour the Homeless**

101 Side Door of Orvieto
Cathedral

103 **Side Door of Orvieto Cathedral** *(detail of Angel)*

102 **Side Door of Orvieto Cathedral,** *(detail: an Angel)*

104 Maquette for Monument to
Pope John XXIII, 1965/66

XIII Monument to Pope John XXIII, 1965/66 *(detail)*

XIV   Monument to Pope John XXIII, 1965/66, *(detail)*

106 Monument to Pope John XXIII,

105 Monument to Pope John XXIII, *(detail of Angels)*

107 Large Crouching Figure II, 1968

108 Large Crouching Figure II, *(back-view)*

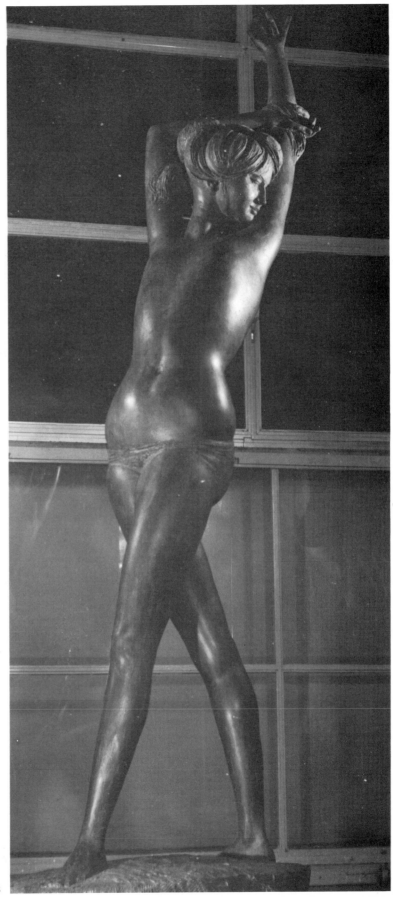

109 Large Bather VII, 1968

110 Large Seated Figure II, 1969

111 Large Seated Figure II, *(detail)*

112 Large Seated Figure II, *(detail)*

113 Head of a Woman, 1949

114 Nanda, 1954

115 Mother and Child, 1950

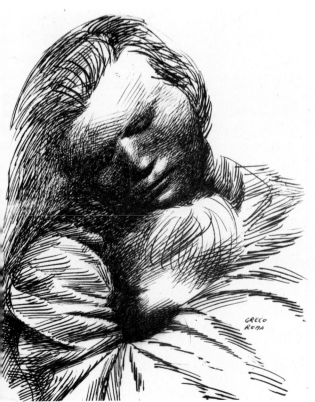

116 Head and Shoulders of a Girl, 1950   117 Drawing, 1957

119   Nude, 1954

120 Nude, 1954

122 Drawing, 1950

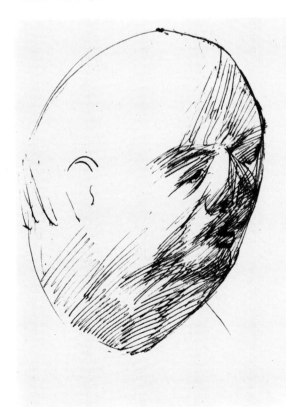

121 Portrait, 1948

123   The Good Shepherd, 1953

124 Portrait of J.P. Hodin, 1965

125 Portrait of J.P. Hodin, 1964

126 Lovers, 1961

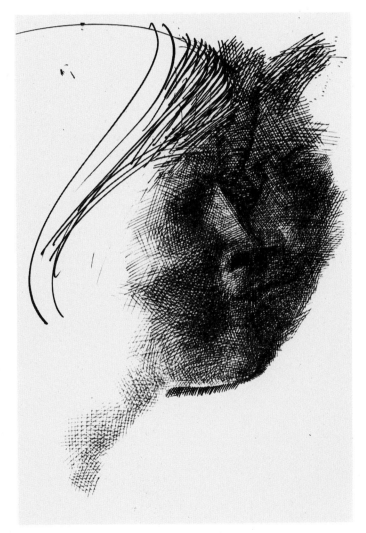

127   Kiss, 1962

128   Head of a Man, 1953

129   Sleeping Fisherman, 1954

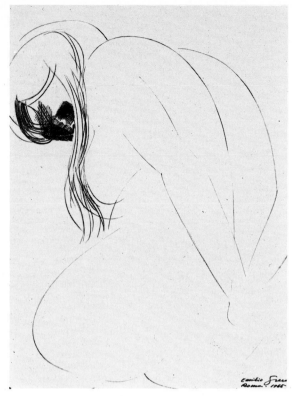

130   Torso, 1965

131   Nude, 1965

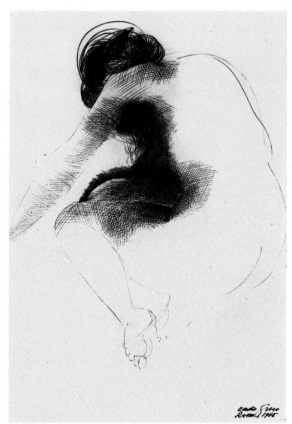

132   Nude, 1954

133   Crouching Nude, 1965

135   In Mood of Debussy, 1965

134   Recling Nude, 1960

138 Nude, 1960

136 Annabelle, 1965

137 Nicole, 1965

139 Girl Coming Out of the Bath, 1963

140 Abandon, 1965

141 Annabelle, 1965

142 Drawing, 1953

144 In Mood of Bach, 1954

143 Portrait, 1961

145 Girl, 1960

146 Annabelle, 1965

147 Claudia, 1963

148 Dog, 1961

150 Study of Pinocchio, 1953

149 Study of Large Bather, 1956

151 Study of Pinocchio, 1953

152 Sketch for the Monument
'The Elevation of the Soul of Man', 1956

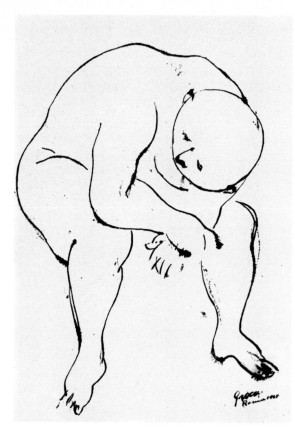

153 Wrestler, 1948

155 St John and Christ, 1959. Illustration for Dante's 'Divine Comedy', Paradiso, Canto XXVI

154 Portrait of Pope John XXIII, 1962. Study for Centre Door of Orvieto Cathedral

156 Thaïs, 1958, Illustration for Dante's 'Divine Comedy', Inferno, Canto XVIII

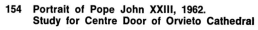

157 Bust of a Young Woman, 1961

158 Woman Combing her hair, 1961

159 Erica, 1961

160 Illustration for Ovid's *Ars Amatoria,* **1968**

161 Illustration for Ovid's *Ars Amatoria,* **1968**

Acknowledgements to the Photographs

Illustrations in the Text

G. Gherardi – A. Fiorelli, Rome: 10, 14, 15
Oscar Savio, Aventino: 5, 6, 7, 8, 9, 11, 12, 13

Monochrome Plates

A. Cartoni, Rome: 14, 15, 19, 27, 115, 120, 142
Cesare Barzacchi, Pisa: 64, 107, 109, 110, 111, 112
Ferretti: 7, 15
Foto Barzacchi: 20
Fotocelere, Turin: 69
Foto Giacomelli, Venice: 21, 29, 30, 54, 62

Foto Grassi, Siena: 18
Foto Greco: 5, 25, 26, 31, 32, 33, 35, 36, 41, 46, 56, 57, 67, 74, 76
Fotorapida, Terni: 93
FotoRotoGrafica, Terni: 92
Foto Savio, Rome: 37, 38
G. Gherardi – A. Fiorelli, Rome: 3, 49, 83, 91, 94, 95, 96, 97, 99, 100, 103, 113, 117, 119, 121, 123, 126, 127, 128, 132, 134, 138, 143, 144, 145, 147, 148, 149, 150, 151, 152, 154, 156, 157, 158
Giannini & Serto, Rome: 86
Michele Como, Rome: 6, 44
Oscar Savio, Aventino: 58, 65, 68, 130
Peter Stükl, Munich: 1, 43